Syrian Refugees, Applied Theater, Workshop Facilitation, and Stories

This book analyzes and theorizes the efficacy of using applied theater as a tool to address refugee issues of displacement, trauma, adjustment, and psychological well-being, in addition to split community belonging.

Fadi Skeiker connects refugee narratives to the themes of imagination, home, gender, and conservatism, among others. Each chapter outlines the author's applied theater practice, as a Syrian, with and for Syrian refugees in the countries of Jordan, Germany, and the United States.

This book will be of great interest to scholars, students, and practitioners of applied theater studies and refugee studies.

Fadi Skeiker is Associate Professor of Theater Arts at The University of the Arts, Philadelphia, USA.

Syrian Refugees, Applied Theater, Workshop Facilitation, and Stories

While They Were Waiting

Fadi Skeiker

Routledge
Taylor & Francis Group

LONDON AND NEW YORK

First published 2021
by Routledge
2 Park Square, Milton Park, Abingdon, Oxon OX14 4RN

and by Routledge
605 Third Avenue, New York, NY 10017

First issued in paperback 2022

Routledge is an imprint of the Taylor & Francis Group, an informa business

British Library Cataloguing-in-Publication Data
A catalogue record for this book is available from the British Library

Library of Congress Cataloging-in-Publication Data
A catalog record for this book has been requested

ISBN: 978-0-367-65405-4 (pbk)
ISBN: 978-0-367-46952-8 (hbk)
ISBN: 978-1-003-03218-2 (ebk)

DOI: 10.4324/9781003032182

Typeset in Times New Roman
by Apex CoVantage, LLC

I dedicate this book to Fayad, Raghda, Lida, Amer, Dima, Kinda, Kinana, Alexander, Julian, Alex, Malin, Rafael, Kipland, Julia, Raymond, and Addison.

For my thoughtful and loving wife, Myla, and my child, Aram.

I also dedicate this book to refugees who were or were not part of this book, and to all applied theater practitioners who work with and for refugees.

Contents

Foreword: in search of imagination

In 1992, I walked into Healthcare for the Homeless, a confidential clinic for homeless men and women living with HIV in Washington, DC. I had been invited to lead some theater workshops with clients at the clinic. I was 24 years old. I had no experience working with homeless populations, nor had I any experiences with people living with HIV. My theater background was fairly traditional. I was an actor, a director, and an improviser, and I had taught theater workshops at some summer camps and high schools. Applied theater was not a field. It was not yet a term, as far as I knew.

Upon arriving at the scheduled time for my first workshop at the clinic, I found an empty room. An hour later, it was still empty.

The next week, it was the same.

And the next.

But the fourth week (and though I want to give myself credit for persistence, the truth is, my ego would not let me give up), one man was sitting in the room when I arrived.

Russell.

He asked me if I would be back the next week. I said yes.

He said, "Alright. I'll see you next week."

And he left.

The next week, Russell was there. But he wasn't alone.

He was in the company of other men and women who, like him, had complicated relationships to home, to health, and to their own bodies as a still frustratingly unknowable illness changed them from the inside out.

That afternoon, that session, was the beginning of the next stage of my professional, creative, and personal journey. In that room, with Russell and Tim and Jerry, I began to learn about showing up. I began to learn about what a room needs to hold safe and brave. And I began to learn about the mysterious and unsurpassable potential that imagination holds in different lives at shared moments.

I write this foreword
in the summer of 2020
in the midst of the global coronavirus pandemic
as Black Lives Matter redefines U.S. discourse on race and
inspires worldwide protests around social justice.

I write this foreword
as a 53-year-old white, Jewish man: a father, husband, educator,
artist, facilitator, and designer of community process
as the grandchild of immigrants
as a person whose privilege – whose jobs, house, and quality
of life – benefits from and is inextricably bound to a nation's
economy built on the slaughter of Indigenous peoples and the
abduction and enslavement of African peoples.

I start this foreword with context –
moments. Identity, history, and unresolvable complication.
I start here because Fadi Skeiker has demanded that I consider
context if I plan to consider applied theater. His applied theater.

Syrian Refugees, Applied Theater, Workshop Facilitation, and Stories: While They Were Waiting is three things. Well, it's many things. But I believe it is, especially, three things.

First, it's a great read. In Fadi himself, it delivers the reader a thoughtful but not infallible narrator. History and context are clearly laid out, but rather than get lost in the immense details of nations and ideologies, Fadi lands us in (among other places) Zataari Camp in Jordan alongside Syrian refugees whose lives have been forever altered by forces outside their control. He acts as a guide to places and events that demonstrate the thoroughly heartbreaking repercussions of an incredibly complex geopolitical and religious conflict while simultaneously offering us glimpses of joy and creativity. It's a great read.

Second, it's as strong a look on the work of facilitation in applied theater as I have ever read. Fadi not only describes the groups he leads and the people he comes to know with clarity, compassion, and detail, but he also discusses, with the same precision and generosity, what he did. He writes about goals. He writes about building partnerships and recruiting participants. He writes about the activities he plans, and he writes about the moments when he shifts direction to make certain he leads work that is useful and constructive for the participants who have chosen to be present and vulnerable. It's a strong companion for anyone leading in applied theater contexts.

And third, it's a bracing interrogation of and testament to the power of imagination. Fadi invites the reader to imagine so many things – the circumstance of losing your personal and cultural and historic place; the condition of living in a new and unfamiliar world; the experience of waiting, and waiting, helplessly, for bureaucracy and politics to allow your family to move from one unknown to another. Can one imagine these things? Is it appropriate to use global tragedy, as heard in a workshop, as a narrative tool for empathy? These questions, which to me float above and beneath the experience of reading this book, serve as a mirror for the journey Fadi himself seems to take as he spends years in Jordan, in Germany, and eventually in Philadelphia, asking himself what his role is as an applied theater practitioner working with human beings who are enduring the trials of war and exile. He spends these pages describing how he deployed imagination as a weapon for healing. He battles trauma, dislocation, and anxiety with an arsenal comprised entirely of activities that aim acts of creation at the aftermath of campaigns of destruction. Imagination, in Fadi's work, and in the work of this book, has the unflagging mission of expanding the possible – the possible avenues in building a new life for oneself as well as the possible applications for theater as a practice of survival.

My own work has long been consumed by a pursuit of how to utilize the spectacle of expressed imagination to encourage and support imaginative capacity in those I teach, facilitate, and encounter. In my practice, this has led to a focus on process, its design, and its execution. I think a lot about how a well-crafted process can help people imagine more freely, frequently, and boldly. I believe that's more important today than ever before. We are in desperate need of imaginative, collaborative approaches to envision our collective way out of dysfunctional democracy, cutthroat capitalism, systemic racism, and public health crises. In the microcosm of refugee camps, Fadi has been practicing (humbly and without savior delusions) this dangerous work of building community and restoring self. He has been mapping scars – scars that run deep, from the political to the personal. He makes the case that scars are bound to steps forward. That one can't map the future without a cartography of what comes before. That to imagine, one has to look, or at least take brave glances, at where one imagines from. His commitment to the people with whom he works, and to how he conducts that work, runs across every page of this book.

If, in 1992, before walking into Healthcare for the Homeless, I had read *Syrian Refugees, Applied Theater, Workshop Facilitation, and Stories: While They Were Waiting*, I would have been prepared so differently for what lay ahead. Having read it now, in 2020, I am more prepared for the next project I take on, the next workshop I lead, the next process I design. I am more prepared, myself, to imagine what comes next.

Michael Rohd
Phoenix, Arizona
July 2020

Introduction

Prologue

As a theater artist, academic, and social worker, I have found out that very few people understand the practice of applied theater. Questions that I consistently face from my peers in related fields are: *Is this theater? Is this social work? Is it both?* Occasionally, there are more divisive questions arise, such as: *Is it art?* or *Why don't you do aesthetic theater instead?* This division exists in one form or another within each of the theater communities in which I have engaged, from Jordan to Germany, Portugal, and the U.S. Within the fields of theater and social work, projects focusing on applied theater and social issues are looked upon as secondary to the supposed core work of the discipline. For example, within the sub-discipline of performance, applied theater is looked at as of lesser importance than aesthetic theater. Likewise, within social work, a field that is built on the practice, theoreticians are held in more esteem than practitioners.

I argue that this division between theory and practice in social work, and between aesthetic theater and applied theater studies is not only counterproductive, but also dangerous and threatening to the practice and access of democracy in our local communities and academic institutions. Sometimes, I do not even believe that we are still giving voice to this dichotomy, as these issues should have been settled long ago. However, they weren't, and here, nearly a quarter of the way through the twenty-first century, I find myself addressing an unnecessary debate, particularly in academic settings where broadening the interdisciplinary nature of our work and practice, in general, is a necessity. Working together to bridge the gap between the aesthetics and the applied, and between theory and practice, only serves to enhance our goal of promoting acceptance within communities and advancing our pursuit of democratic education and liberal arts practices. Those of us with hybrid professional identities, who are working on the fringe of disciplines, and whose work is interdisciplinary at its core can hardly afford to isolate our practice by putting it into one category or the other.

While this book can be read as a personal account for my applied theater practice with refugees on three continents, it also can be read as an approachable recipe for connecting the aesthetics and the applied, for connecting theory and practice, and ultimately for connecting the arts and social justice. In this book, I share my own accounts conducting applied theater with and for refugees, and meanwhile, I try to trouble the aforementioned dichotomy that has been established in the field of theater studies in particular.

My wish is for this book to mediate the tensions present in theater studies, since it is my basic domain of work. For whatever reason, that kind of meditation has become part and parcel of my professional practice. My own theater practices, both the aesthetic and applied, have always been informed by theories, though not necessarily performance theories. Early on, I found myself borrowing from cultural studies, gender studies, Middle Eastern studies, and identity studies, among others. My unique position as someone with a hybrid identity, a Syrian with a U.S. graduate education, and one who has worked in different institutions, though always as the "other," has allowed me to advocate for and explore disciplines that many of my colleagues believe lay outside the heart of theater studies in general.

For example, while I was serving as Associate Professor and Assistant Dean of the College at the University of Jordan, I advocated for the offering of a theater education course. Toward this effort, I facilitated a partnership with different schools, a move that was perceived as unnecessary by my fellow theater professors and artists. Those naysayers believed that our work as theater faculty should focus solely on preparing the theater artist, as if doing so requires neglecting the practical application of theater in schools. I disagreed then, and I do even more so now that I have seen the positive, life-affirming, and potentially life-changing effects that theater can have outside the context of public performance.

While still in Jordan, I led many applied theater workshops with refugees. Some of them are documented in this book. My work there was, and almost ten years later continues to be, supported by international organizations. At one point, I sought additional assistance from a granting committee organized by the Dean of Academic Affairs. That committee, which had no theater faculty among its number, agreed to support this work. I knew, however, that had I approached my colleagues in theater, they would have rejected my proposal for its lack of connection to aesthetic practice. Later, when I was serving as a visiting associate professor at the University of Minho in Portugal, I also facilitated a short-term project for refugees with a group of my acting students, but my Portuguese students were always questioning the artistry of their practice with refugees, and they continued to perceived themselves as theater artists doing voluntary work but not as theater artists practicing art in a different context.

Part of the resistance against applied work is also related to the corporatization of our academic institutions. More and more we see our academic and even arts-based universities following a corporate model. I am interested in learning how we can continue offering progressive education while simultaneously navigating the increasingly corporate nature of our academic settings. Students in the corporate model have begun to look at a university degree as the ticket that will allow them to enter the consumer culture, and the only way to enter the consumer culture successfully is to follow the rules of the market, earn a degree, and find a job. In this model, performance faculty are tasked with putting creativity and innovation aside to focus on teaching students tap dance and method acting, and most importantly, getting them ready to go to Broadway. It can be difficult to advance applied practice when the demands of the market are so rigidly constructed.

In this climate, I consider myself to be the twice-lucky winner of the fellowship and job market lottery: once when I was a visiting researcher at Free University of Berlin and second in my current position at The University of the Arts in Philadelphia. While in Berlin, I received a fellowship from the EU to do applied theater work with Syrian refugees there. Likewise, my home university has been extremely welcoming to my work with refugees. I do not look at these small successes as a sign of a change in academia in general since in both instances the enthusiasm was attributed to a timely topic and to the fact that I am Syrian myself. In the first instance, the EU felt the need to fund my work; and in the second, my home university is a small, intimate, and community-based institution that encourages innovation in the arts.

Ultimately, those of us actively engaged in applied theater work need to continue documenting our work and advocating for the respect of our peers, whether that be in the fields of theater, social work, or arts therapy in general. As this book demonstrates, applied theater work, particularly among oppressed or otherwise disenfranchised persons, can offer a unique avenue for emotional healing, social integration, and personal advancement.

Applied theater in the Middle East

Applied theater entails planning, executing, and evaluating theater workshops for specific communities, with the ultimate goal being to open a dialogue about the particular issues the community is grappling with. Some applied theater workshops culminate in a public performance that is shared with the general community members. The vast majority of applied theater workshops, however, start and end within the workshop format. The workshop is designed and enacted for the benefit of the participants, never for the benefit of a viewing audience, and before leading an applied theater workshop, a facilitator should consistently ask questions related to his or her own privilege in the context of the workshop, considering how to consciously avoid steering the conversation toward values or topics that might not be authentic to the community.

Before the refugee crisis in 2011, most applied theater programs located in the Middle East had been focusing on women's empowerment, an already controversial topic within the context of a predominantly conservative Arab community. The topic is touchy because many Arabs believe that women are already empowered in their communities. Further, they are resistant to the idea that applied theater projects that focused on women's empowerment were either funded by Western organizations or facilitated by Westerners. Support for this issue in particular is deemed hypocritical, as Arabs do not necessarily consider Western women to be empowered themselves, and they may believe that Westerners should be working on issues within their own communities instead of supporting socio-political work in communities with which they are not familiar. Despite being Middle Eastern myself and fully aware of the specificities of Middle Eastern culture, I witnessed this tension firsthand while leading applied theater workshops with women in the Middle East, and it can be largely attributed to the classic colonial notion of Westerners doing social justice or missionary work in a Global South setting.

Right after 2011, however, the focus of applied theater projects in the Middle East quickly shifted focus from women's rights to refugees, as Syrian refugees scattered to all corners of the Middle East, Turkey, and Europe. Since that time, millions of Syrians have been living in nearby Jordan, Lebanon, and Turkey. Some live in isolated refugee camps such as Zaatari Camp, though the majority of Syrian refugees are living in poverty pockets and conservative neighborhoods. The movement of applied theater work to serving refugees instead of locals was a direct response to the dire need of refugees and the generally unwelcoming environment that they were facing from their local hosts. However, the focus on serving refugees only and ignoring host communities was not without consequences. In fact, it led to a backlash in some communities and prompted increased discrimination against refugees. As a result, applied theater work with refugees began hosting both local community members and refugees to facilitate a dialogue between both parties.

Applied theater and refugees

The refugee presence in host countries, from the Middle East to the United States, has become an excuse for right-wing politicians and media outlets to launch attacks on progressive advocacy for displaced people, particularly those who are the victims of global political and human rights crises. This book offers a counter narrative and attempts to create forums conceived by applied theater techniques that may incite conversation about the personal narratives of refugees and foster the kind of productive dialogue that should exist between refugees and the host communities.

In trying to heal the traumas refugees have experienced while living in and escaping a war zone, the Western approach might be to recommend traditional therapy. The scale of refugee communities and centers, and the cultural context of Arab communities, makes this an unlikely, impractical solution, though. Applied theater is one of the few alternative practices that can safely address the trauma that refugees have encountered yet invites them to rationally and emotionally process their current situations. The therapeutic dimensions of applied theater are far less invasive than traditional therapy, and it is more likely for a refugee to attend an applied theater workshop than to go to a traditional therapy session. This is, at least, the case for Syrian refugees who come from communities in which going to a therapist might carry negative social stigma. In addition, applied theater is one of the few platforms where a group of refugees might forge ephemeral community bonds, where they are given the time together to remap their trauma, collectively dialogue, contest ideas about their lives as refugees, and hope for a better future.

During an applied theater workshop, practical applications of social work, therapy, community organizing, arts, and other disciplines are all at play. In my own practice, and as I document in the chapters that follow, I use applied theater to facilitate theater arts and community organizing within the theoretical lenses of identity studies and diasporic studies, among others. These theories are present in my head while planning for my work, but the minute I enter the room to lead a workshop, I remind myself that what matters in my practice is not to follow the theory rigidly but rather to focus on the group of people I am working with. I am in the workshops for them and must balance creating a community with paying individual attention to each and every person in the group.

In this book, I take you on a journey with me to my applied theater workshops in three episodes or global locations. I introduce you to narratives that refugees have shared, both with me in social interaction and within the workshop setting. Each of these individuals has struggled to create a new normalcy in their lives while living in a strange home. You will witness them playing applied theater games that will help them to open up, discuss, dialogue, and envision better versions for their futures. You will also hear words of frustration, discouragement, and trauma.

Chapter 1, "Theory, Issues, and Stories: Context," charts my journey into conducting applied theater workshops with refugees in Jordan. The chapter notes, specifically, my field observations on gender dynamics and conservatism within the context of the Middle East. I find this important since it will build understanding and produce knowledge that is most needed when conducting applied theater work with refugees in the West. It is important to note that most of the refugees in the West are from Global South countries where conservatism is the norm and where gender dynamics are uniquely different from those in the West. In addition, the chapter tackles the nuts and bolts of applied theater practice while addressing specific concepts such as empathy, reflection, and the role of the facilitator.

Chapter 2, "Jordan: Youth, Gender, and Discovering the Individual," argues that the use of identity narratives in applied theater practice can be a road map to assist refugees when they are newly transplanted in their host community. In this chapter, I introduce the reader to three female refugee youths from Syria. Each of the young women participated in workshops for young people that I hosted in Jordan during which we focused on developing personal narratives. The chapter introduces the monologue as an excellent platform for empowering refugees and workshop participants in the exploration of how individual stories are experienced differently from the homogenized global discourse on refugee experience.

Chapter 3, "Germany: Organizing and Facilitating a Workshop," presents my work with a diverse group of all-male refugees from different Global South countries who were living in a refugee transitional center in Hamburg in 2015. The chapter focuses specifically on creating group narratives, both verbal and physical. Additionally, the chapter presents tactics for starting a refugee workshop and work involved in materializing this particular set of sessions.

Chapter 4, "The United States: Serving the Refugee, Connecting with the Community," addresses my work for and with refugees in Philadelphia, a third and equally unique context compared with those of Jordan and Germany. In Philadelphia, I collaborated with HIAS, a government-funded, privately operated organization that focuses on assisting newly arrived refugees to integrate into the U.S. The chapter explores practical questions about drama therapy and its implication within the context of applied theater workshops. Other questions that are tackled in this chapter are those of aesthetic theater versus applied theater in addition to the roles of movement and physicality in applied theater.

In the conclusion, I decided to further unpack some of the shared themes that rose to the surface of my work in each of the three global contexts and locations. I focus, in particular, on the role of empowerment, the narrative (both individual and group narrative), the refugee as a stranger, and the concept of diaspora. I end the conclusion with the three *musts* that I adhere to whenever I lead this kind of work.

In both contexts, Western and Middle Eastern, the current political climate fosters a public discourse that often attacks refugee resettlement. Under these conditions, it is important for progressive, applied theater scholars/practitioners to stand together, form coalitions, and work in community. Practicing applied theater with and for refugees is some of the most demanding work that an applied theater artist can do, and quite simply, we need more resources to master our craft within the workshop setting. Only this will support a theoretical foundation that will help to better shape and push our discipline. The connection between theory and practice is needed in this emerging field, and it is incumbent upon us to shape the field so that it can better serve vulnerable communities.

Multiple narratives, same narrative

This book offers insights on my personal work with and for Syrian refugees in three countries. Despite the relatively extensive studies that tackle the relationship between artists and refugees, I leverage my own existence as a Syrian artist/academic/scholar to offer a unique and unparalleled view of an insider performing what is typically outsiders' work. My background, in many cases, provided me quick and trusted access to workshop participants, and at the time, I was conducting much of this work out of a general desire to practice without intention to publish. As I deepened and expanded my work, my academic standing offered the right amount of distancing to critically reflect on these experiences.

While my case studies are based in three countries, the implication of the research is global. The inspiring stories that are presented in the book, while personal, subjective, and detailed, are reflected in stories of the oppressed from all over the world. Globally, marginalized communities share a sense of unity in their struggle against forces of international domination. Not only is the struggle one, the suffering is also one. But the hope is one as well. If you read this text and pay special attention to the personal narratives shared by refugees, you may feel that the multiple stories of the refugees flow as if they are the story of one single refugee. As I highlight in later chapters, the refugee narrative is similar despite his or her nation of geographic origin. The host community members also share a single narrative despite the different geography. Further, there is a shared dynamic between refugees and the host community. This dynamic is almost the same regardless of where the refugees come from or where the host community is located. In general, the central relevance, therefore, is that most displaced persons struggle to suppress the trauma of seeking refuge while simultaneously learning to integrate into a new, foreign culture. All the while, they are attempting to preserve life-affirming ties to their family, friends, and the culture that they have left behind. They are behaving sociologically on multiple levels, and their minds, souls, and hearts are divided between homeland and host community.

This book can be read on many levels. It can be read as an academic book, as a memoir, as a journalistic piece, and even as creative non-fiction. Most of the knowledge produced in this book is derived from my applied theater workshops, conversations, public talks, etc. But all in all, I feel that this book is actually about me and my fellow Syrians. Though I did not directly experience violent displacement, my unique situation as a Syrian applied theater practitioner/artist/academic leading applied theater workshops with Syrian refugees is unique for both them and me. While writing I use the personal narrative form to open windows to my own story. However, the refugee voices are always central to the narrative. Though told from my point of view, this is their book, these are their stories, and the work is in service of their betterment. It is also very important for me to point out that I am not using their narratives, stories, and voices as tokens to prove a point or to argue, but I intentionally invite them to be part and parcel of the discourse on refugee resettlement and healing.

1 Theory, issues, and stories
Context

At the beginning of the Syrian refugee crisis in 2011, few international organizations were cognizant of the need for psycho-social support among refugees, as most of them were heavily concerned with providing food, water, tents, blankets, and other life essentials to the refugees who were at the time pouring across Syrian borders and into neighboring countries. This was, at the time, one of a series of ongoing regional conflicts. Iraq, to Syria's east, has struggled through internal violence since the American invasion in 2003, and in this most recent round, Syria, Egypt, Gaza, and Palestine were simultaneously weathering a period of unrest best known as the Arab Spring. Jordan has been named the Switzerland of the Middle East since it is the only country in the region that did not suffer the horrors of war the same way almost all of its neighboring countries had. In the Middle East, Jordan is the only country that has been relatively stable, both socially and politically, and since it kept its borders open throughout 2011, many refugees who left neighboring countries found in Jordan a place to catch their breath before they might leave for somewhere else.

Syrianhood as an identity construct is similar to any identity, not only informed by what persons think about themselves, but also by what others perceive of them as well. In a 2020 report from the German Institute for International and Security Affairs, Suat Kinikliogu found that in Turkey, where in excess of five million Syrians have migrated, "negative public perceptions toward [Syrian] refugees have grown significantly. Although incidences of violence have been negligible, numerous public opinion polls confirm a stark decline in public support for hosting the refugees" (1).

This shift in the way a Syrianhood is perceived is not restricted to Turkey. For someone like me, a Syrian living in Jordan throughout the refugee crisis, it was easy to notice the change in the way Jordanians perceived us Syrians. I moved to Jordan in 2010 after finishing my Ph.D. at The University of Texas at Austin. I had always been curious about Jordan and was excited to receive my first academic appointment at The University of Jordan. In 2010, when I first arrived in Amman, Syrians were described as "kind," "intellectual," or "artistic," but by 2011 they were being described as unwanted and disruptive. The negative discourse surrounding Syrians has continued since that time, and it informs how Syrians living in Jordan perceive themselves, as they have become the focal point of an old/new human catastrophe called the refugee crisis.

Let's travel in time to 2011 and walk in the streets of Amman, a beautiful city that is built in the middle of seven mountains, a city unique for the stairs that connect its neighborhoods. In Amman, you hear all kinds of accents, most notably Iraqi, Egyptian, Palestinian, and now Syrian.

In addition to its eastern Jordanians, Jordan is a land composed mostly of second-generation refugees from Palestine and displaced Iraqis; in 2011 it was about to host a new wave, this time Syrians. The pre-existing refugee communities in Jordan were about to increase. Most early refugees came running away from war, millions of them, starting from Palestine in two major waves in 1948 and 1967. Recently, and since 2011, the United Nations High Commissioner for Refugees (UNHCR) has claimed the official presence of about 655,000 Syrians in Jordan; however, unofficial numbers predict that up to two million Syrians may be residing there. The numbers are staggering, with about 139,000 of the Syrians living in the Zaatari and Azraq camps (UNHCR, 2020).

At the time that the 2011 crisis emerged, I was happily settled in Jordan, living as a Syrian academic/artist teaching theater at The University of Jordan. At the time I had developed an interest in applied theater and – in addition to my teaching and directing practices – had started leading applied theater workshops and other projects, both locally in Jordan and regionally in Egypt and Lebanon. I had also started publishing about my applied theater work. Imagine my confusion and surprise as my fellow countrymen fled our home by the tens of thousands into a neighboring nation where I was living a comfortable existence. Gone were my weekend trips across the border to visit my family, and a new perception of what it meant to be Syrian in Jordan (and across the Middle East) emerged. In light of the circumstances, I believed it was my best option to use my training to work with other Syrians in the best way I knew how: using theater as a tool for change.

Applied theater field in Jordan

In 2011, I wrote my first article detailing applied theater work I had been conducting with Palestinian refugees in Jordan (Skeiker, 2011). In that article, I argued that the idea of theater as "applied" was not familiar to people in Jordan because most of the work taking place at the time, even in refugee camps and in community centers, revolved around preparing a performance and presenting it to the camp residents. The idea of leading a workshop solely to empower the participants, without thinking about a final product or a public presentation, was uncommon. Many things have changed since then, and it is now difficult to map out all of the exciting projects that are applied in nature and conducted with Syrian refugees in Jordan and the Middle East.

I now think of the time between 2011 and 2015 as a period of explosive interest in the potentials of art therapy, drama therapy, and applied theater as an umbrella for some of those practices. In that window, I saw how eager both refugees and organizations serving them were to try something new and potentially life altering. Reflecting on my own applied theater practices with refugees between 2011 and now, I notice a shift in the way refugee workshop participants respond to my workshops, and I even notice a shift in the way I lead my workshops. In a nutshell, I could summarize the changes with the following points.

- In 2011, workshop participants, mostly Syrian refugees in Jordan, were using applied theater workshops to practice building a public narrative (Ganz, 2011), premised on their individual stories, toward a collective cry for freedom. In 2015, the discourse of the workshop participants was focused on their desire to move to Europe.
- In 2011, my applied theater practice culminated in public presentations, but by 2015 having such public presentations was no longer a consideration.
- In 2011, workshop participants' narratives most often described confrontations between peaceful changing forces and violent regime forces, while participants in 2015 mostly described struggles related to their refugee journeys.

Over the span of four years, the reasons for refugees' fleeing shifted from being aligned with one political party or the other to simply escaping circumstances that were dangerous for anyone, regardless of party or affiliation. Similarly, my approach shifted from product-oriented work to process-oriented work. It is difficult for me to determine how the shift happened. It is either that the tragedy became too immense to handle in a performance, or that my practice evolved and participants allowed themselves to share stories so personal in nature that I could not ask them – nor did I want to ask them – to share them publicly. Maybe it is both.

As my practice was changing, so was the field of applied theater in the Middle East. This change can be credited to the social workers, first and foremost, who reached a dead end in their practice and wanted to learn new skills that would allow them to engage their clients. More change came also from non-governmental organizations (NGOs) which were allocating funds to do arts work that is "applied" in nature and is not necessarily geared toward having a final artistic product. Combined, the discovery of applied arts in the field of social work and the availability of funding for these projects through NGOs led to a fortuitous combination of will and way, particularly in Jordan where Zaatari Camp was forming, and it seemed that the "weigh station" that it was intended to be was actually shaping into a permanent "city" of its own.

Zaatari Camp

Zaatari Refugee Camp is located in Jordan just two miles across the Syrian border. It was established to accommodate the influx of Syrian refugees who crossed into Jordan after 2011. The camp is a vast, fenced-in land in the middle of the desert where thousands of tents were installed to house tens of thousands of families fleeing the Syrian war. The majority of families living in Zaatari are refugees from the southern part of Syria. This region of Syria is very conservative and tribal, with blood kinship as the dictating factor of their social and even political habitus (Tiltnes, Zhang, & Pedersen, 2019). Art, except for TV series drama, was very limited in their lives.

While residing in Zaatari Camp under very unwelcoming physical conditions (dust, tents, and later, caravans), and facing the challenges of psychological stress, depression, and anxiety among others (Al-Krenawi, 2019), most refugees, and especially teens, are encouraged to participate in one of the arts-based psycho-social support activities that are held within one of the many international organization sites that are located inside the camp. Many refugees decide to engage with these activities because they are bored. Quite simply, they have little or nothing to do in the camp. A secondary reason may be that some of them assume that if they participate in these activities, they will get more "points," which will help them to be selected for transfer as legal refugees to the west of Jordan. Finally, participating in these activities allows them to make connections with foreigners who are either working for the international organizations or leading the artistic projects.

Regardless of the reasons that entice refugees to join these applied arts projects, their participation is intended to have both short- and long-term effects. In the short run, participants exit more empowered than when they entered. Many of these projects are structured around giving participants small, easily executable tasks that allow them to immediately see the result of their work. Also, most arts-based workshop activities include participants with no tribal or religious connection whatsoever. The only commonality among participants is their shared refugee experiences. These workshops allow them to sit together, talk, converse, and exchange ideas about their stories, while they are simultaneously engaged in an artistic practice that can be related to their experiences or not. Thus, their social connection is strengthened through prolonged exposure and the exchange of intimate dialogue.

In the early years of the refugee crisis, these small and short workshops were influential in creating new social ties among refugees. Such ties and connections overcome the conservative, tribal bonds that depended on religion, families, and gender. In such workshops, many refugees experience socializing with others from outside their tribe, religion, and sometimes gender community for the first time. For many of them, it is the first time participating in an event that resists the conservative nature of the way they were brought up.

Conservatism and applied theater

Arab communities are predominantly religious and conservative. This conservatism presents most clearly in the public sphere of a typical Arab city or town. It is visible in how gender is performed in the street. Women cover their bodies, male catcalling is the norm, and public affection is rare and frowned upon. People are almost never found holding hands. Random pedestrians are empowered by male privilege and anonymity, allowing them to feel free to comment on women's appearance and clothing without fear of being questioned. The interference is not limited only to catcalling but can also include commenting on a woman's not wearing hijab or addressing her in derogatory terms related to her gender.

I recall once leading a workshop on gender equality among refugees in Amman, Jordan, in 2014. The workshop participants were refugees from different Arab countries who were residing in Jordan. With them was a group of social activists who work with refugees. I ran the workshop as I normally would when conducting applied theater work. I asked the participants to recall stories of when they felt gender played a role in their life decisions, and then I asked them to dramatize those stories and reflect on them.

While in the middle of the exercise, one of the participants expressed his contempt, complaining that the talk around gender equality in the Arab world is overrated. He defended his position by arguing that in the Arab world men and women are equally paid, while most Western countries are still struggling on that front. The young man also mentioned that the percentage of women who hold powerful political and economic positions in the

Arab world is similar to that in Western countries. He continued by saying that all of this emphasis on gender equality is part of a Western conspiracy agenda to culturally invade the fabric of Arab society. In the face of such an incident, and as a facilitator, I struggled with how to progress. I knew that as a practitioner I needed to do the following: 1) give him time to express his thoughts, which I did; 2) hear his argument and try to understand where he was coming from, which I also did; and 3) try not to take sides.

Workshops such as that one which are supported by international organizations tend to attract social activists from around the Arab world. Similarly, they are typically attended by like-minded Arab youth who are eager to change the male-centered and patriarchal dynamics that pervade Arab communities. In the aforementioned workshop, and in consideration of the population, I decided to take that moment as a teaching opportunity about engaging in dialogue on issues of disagreement. Instead of answering the young conservative man, I decided to direct the question to the group and ask them to respond to him. The others engaged, and the discussion went on. After a while, I began to feel that the dialogue was not winding down. It was about 7 pm, and sunset was looming.

The workshop took place in Al-Balad Theater, one of the few alternative cultural sites in Amman. Al-Balad Theater had the reputation of bringing unique experiences to their audiences and getting audiences to engage in conversations about the arts and community activism. The site is beautifully located on Amman Mountain and very close to downtown Amman where there is a very famous falafel place. To get there from the theater, you descend a beautiful staircase that leads from Amman Mountain directly to downtown. The stone stairway is full of paintings and graffiti reflective of the beauty of Amman, and it is heavily traversed.

I kindly asked the young man and a woman who had been most fiercely engaged in the conversation to participate in a social experiment in which each of them would walk separately down the stairs to downtown and get us falafel from the restaurant. Each would come back and report to us what had happened to them while they walked in the street. The woman was happy to participate in the experiment, whereas the man did not respond at all. The woman accepted knowing that this experiment would prove her right in her argument that gender inequality is something that is most keenly felt in the public sphere (e.g. catcalling, harassment, and a general feeling of unsafety at night in public).

Then, I asked each of them to create a frozen image that represented their understanding of their beliefs, and toward the end, both seemed to understand each other's position. The man understood that when women walk by themselves in public spaces they do not feel safe, and the woman appreciated the man's perspective that solutions should come from within the community and not from imposing agendas funded with foreign-aid dollars.

This situation was similar to another incident that played out in the Jordanian political sphere. Within the Jordanian parliament, one of the most articulate female members of parliament, Hind Al-Fayez, was engaged in a heated discussion with a male parliament member. The discussion grew contentious, with both members arguing fiercely and speaking over each other. The point at hand was not gender related at all, as they were arguing about the national Arab movement. Other parliament members were trying in vain to calm them down when suddenly another male parliament member shouted, "Sit down, Hind!" in an imperative and commanding manner. His demand for her acquiescence went viral on social media as activists took the incident as a signal that however achieved a woman is, and however present she may be in the public sphere, she is still a "woman" in the eyes of a man. He can still order her to "sit down" if he feels that her discourse conflicts with or undermines his own.

I share these stories to provide a fuller context for practicing applied theater in the Middle East in general and to inform the reader of the risks and the minefields that any applied theater practitioner must be willing to cross to make the work happen. In such sensitive situations, applied theater workshop participants are keen to present their side of the stories being discussed and try their best to support their arguments and present their personal truths as the only truth. In such instances, I find myself sharing the view of applied theater scholar James Thompson (2005, p. 28) who claims that the focus should be on the "conjecture" and not the truth. Within that spirit, I believe that the commitment in applied theater practice should not be to agree on a kind of universal truth that a facilitator will feed the participants, but rather that the commitment should be to generate a truth that can work for the targeted group, a truth that is derived from the real stories of the participants and a truth that is not dictated by biased historical information.

This practice informs my third strategy as a facilitator: not to take sides. Intentionally, I do not steer the conversation of an applied theater workshop, even if doing so might serve a political agenda that I might support or oppose. For example, when leading workshops with Syrian refugees, the question of whether a refugee is siding with the regime or the opposition is always there, so I avoid encouraging these kinds of polarizing conversations. Instead, I focus on micro-analyzing the personal stories and connecting them to the public sphere through which participants should see themselves becoming citizens of their new home nations. Whatever "truths" lie within the stories of the participants will reveal themselves in the final performance, whether that be public or solely among the participants themselves.

Applied theater scholar Amanda Fisher (2005) says that the real power of applied theater is in its ability to facilitate the emergence of "truth process." From this perspective, applied theater has a role in moving behind the perceived truth. Through the techniques used, participants can build a better, well-rounded understanding for their situation, "critique" their own positions, and build a critical awareness of themselves. The work of applied theater, as described by Fisher, becomes indeed an "excavation" of the truth as a "process." Truth should be contested/negotiated but never achieved. Applied theater workshops should unsettle convictions during the workshop time and leave the participant in an ambivalent state.

Fisher (2005) also questions the ethical positioning of the facilitator of the applied theater project. Her work builds on that of applied theater scholar James Thompson (2005) in which he describes his work in Sri Lanka as an "ethical minefield." These questionings of facilitator involvement and the ethics of facilitation are so important, especially because the main goal of applied theater is to offer a space for community members to put their ideas of social interaction, and perhaps political views, to the test. The goal should never be to exploit an ulterior mission of the host organization, funding agency, or the leader him/herself.

In an applied theater workshop, the primary goal at the outset is to create "a safe environment" for participants so that they can talk by themselves without being judged. There are many techniques I used to create this safe space; one of them is to dedicate the beginning of the workshop for rule setting. I typically post a flip chart and bring lots of markers and ask participants what would make them feel safe to talk freely; then I go over the list with them and draft an agreement on the conditions and ask them to sign it. Next, I open the workshop by introducing a concept and asking the participants to respond to it. For example, I asked refugees in one workshop to respond to the concepts of courage and fear, describing when they felt fearful or courageous as they were traveling out of Syria.

While I might capitalize on the fact that I am Syrian myself at the outset of a workshop by posing such an intimate question, other applied theater practitioners who are culturally distanced from the group with which they work might take more time to address the personal questions of their targeted group. Applied theater scholar Tim Prentki (2015, p. 29) would go as far as to describe the "gulf" between the participants and facilitator to be "danger[ous]." Having said that, I witnessed an episode where the distance between the participants and the facilitator was helpful in the process of facilitating applied theater projects. I recall here the work of Alexander Schroeder, who is a theater professor at The University of the Arts in Berlin and an applied theater practitioner who formed a theater company composed mostly of Syrian youth refugees in Berlin. Schroeder stayed with the same group of refugees for about two months before they began opening up about their trips. This kind of trust takes time. However, his work was not only related to the time he would spend with them in the applied theater workshop; he also would visit them in their residences at the camp, hang out with them, have coffee with them, and even ask them to help him learn Arabic.

Schroeder's approach relies on not treating refugees as "clients" or "subjects" but as human beings who need locals from the host community to remind them that they are members of the community and that they can and should still participate in a civic and social life within their new neighborhoods, cities, and towns. His work also reminds refugees that their trauma matters. This personal connection between the applied theater artist and the community transcends the traditional applied theater project in that it invites artists to immerse themselves in the life of the refugee/participant community in order to excavate for specifics among the community members, much as an ethnographer would.

Applied theater as embodied knowledge and gender

Applied theater constitutes a sense of embodied knowledge wherein the bodies of those participating in the applied theater workshop become, themselves, the sites where the knowledge is contested, negotiated, and ultimately formed. As I stated earlier, knowledge in this regard should be not connected to finding the "truth" because I actually do not believe that the task of applied theater is to reach a specific truth. On the contrary, I look at the truth as a fluid concept. The only truth I look for during the workshop is a truth of self and the ability to produce a new knowledge that is based on plurality and viewing multiple truths from different perspectives.

In addition to its contribution in knowledge production, embodied knowledge contributes to energizing the workshop site. Embodied knowledge as materialized through frozen images or corporal creations of the group might be interpreted as a perspective that holds an aesthetic value. As well, embodied knowledge transforms the bodies of the participants into physical scripts to be interpreted. Frozen-image performative scores become a site to form a group embodied awareness. In my applied theater workshops, I divide the participants into groups and ask each group to produce an informed frozen image that will carry the weight of their understanding of a specific issue or concept. Their group work will constitute an episode during which they will work out both their bodies and their minds, as they will start by discussing the issue or the concept, and then they will have to collectively come up with a frozen image that will be a symbolic or realistic objective correlative for their thoughts. Participants will respond to a prompt by me, the facilitator, and form a frozen image that is in dialogue physically or metaphorically with the concept. Half of the workshop participants will exhibit their frozen image, and the other half will watch it before they all dialogue about it.

One of the risks that such an approach carries is the male gaze, especially while leading applied theater workshops in conservative communities where both men and women are in the same room together. In that regard, and since the body will be the focal point of attention, both males and females might feel distracted because they are not used to exhibiting the body or regarding it as a site for knowledge production.

In one of the programs I co-led in Jordan, the creative team of the Jordanian branch of Ruwwad and I began working on a project called "My Voice, My Identity." Ruwwad is a Middle Eastern regional organization that focuses on empowering youth and supporting them through social organizing. Part of the work of Ruwwad in Amman is to enact change and empower youth through the arts. The program I was co-leading at the time focused on exploring gender biases among the youth of Ruwwad and attempted to create a new awareness about gender dynamics that might lead to a change in the way men perceive women within this conservative setting.

The youth who participated in that series of workshops came from conservative backgrounds and were mostly college students. The other facilitator, who was a woman, and I divided the participants into two groups according to gender; I led the male group, while Lana led the female group. The program's direct goal was to use theater as a tool to discuss the gender dynamics between men and women within the context of Jabal Al Natheef, one of the most conservative neighborhoods in Amman. We hoped that by making the decision to split the group, it might be easier for the participants to more deeply engage in their discussions when surrounded by those of their same gender. Within the setting of the program, participants would come up with stories and public narratives that were representative of their understanding of the gender dynamics between men and women within their own communities.

At the time, I was translating an extremely interesting book chapter titled "On the Gender Continuum," written by theater scholar Stacy Wolf (2007); it describes a theater exercise designed to explore gender performance in both private and public spheres. I decided to use parts of that exercise. While leading the workshop for men, I asked them to act out *walking down the street in a masculine manner*. One of the men walked across the room. He did not have a specific goal while walking, and he was walking slowly, his chest and shoulders open. He seemed comfortable while strolling and looking around. I then asked the same man to do the same exact walk but while pretending to be a woman. When prompted to walk like a woman, his first impulse was to look in the room for some kind of object. He decided to hold a book, and he brought the book close to his chest. In this pose, his walk was determined and fast.

I asked the young man to explain the two walks and share with the group what they teach us about gender dynamics and the way in which gender plays out in the public sphere in Jordan. The young man stated that while a man can walk in his neighborhood without a purpose other than just walking, on the other hand, a woman's visibility in the public sphere is tied to a specific goal, and the goal of her visibility should be signified by an object. In the case he presented, the object was a book, which signifies that she is either going to school/university or going to study with her friends. The other signifier of her determination was her steady stride, which contrasted with the loose strides that a man can take.

Needless to say, this story does not represent the way in which all Jordanian women walk in public, but it does indicate the way in which a woman is perceived in a conservative neighborhood in Jordan. It is also interesting to contrast a male perception of female behavior with the way in which women in the same community perceive themselves. The women whom I worked with on this project or in other projects in Ruwwad, even though their dress and behavior, adhered to the patriarchal and conservative nature of their surroundings. However, many Jordanian women develop other subtle tactics that allow them to work out the system, as they try to gain small victories to shift the public perception of Arab feminism. For example, many Jordanian women are highly educated. They have gone to universities, and some of them major in disciplines, such as mechanical engineering, that are perceived as "male." Also, many turn to social centers such as Ruwwad to take advantage of the services they provide such as psycho-social support, professional development, and capacity building.

In addition to the normal professional development that centers such as Ruwwad offer, they are also actively involved in public forums where risky ideas are put on the table. The work of Ruwwad is very important in the lives of these youth, both men and women, because they offer a safe space in which new ideas are introduced, contested, and negotiated. In addition, Ruwwad constitutes a counter front against the work of the very active conservative Islamic brotherhood groups which have a very strong presence in the same neighborhood.

The gender continuum exercise represents an extremely important example of an applied theater practice that easily opens a broad discussion on a variety of issues, social/political and personal. In addition, it can easily adapt for utilization in different cultural contexts. In conservative communities where gender roles are strictly defined, it is difficult to imagine alternative ways of living, and the question of imagination becomes crucial because the only way to start a new way of living is to begin by imagining it.

In search of imagination

I once started a workshop in Jordan with a simple question: *If you had all the resources you could need, how would you imagine your life to be?* I remember how difficult it was for some participants, especially those who were facing economic challenges, to even imagine themselves in different or better positions. Their answers were either that they would own an apartment or a car, and/or that they would get married. No one said, for example, that they imagined having an apartment on the moon, that they would write a novel that would be turned into an Oscar-winning movie, or that they possessed the magical ability to fly. No one even imagined being able to end the war and promote regional peace.

The search for imagination in applied theater work will be different in each setting, as the aspirations of groups and communities, even in the context of the Arab world, are not monolithic. A woman trapped in a conservative community may aspire to live in a society that is equal; a young man who is bullied in school will aspire toward a safe learning environment; and a refugee trapped in her trauma will hope to be able to move beyond her refugee story and exercise control over her life again.

Imagination is not just essential for enhancing learning and comprehension in academic settings (Fiorella & Mayer, 2015, pp. 84–94). The inability to imagine is also an indication of the limitations to enacting change in some communities. I believe that to create social and personal change, we need first to train community members to imagine that these things are possible. Applied theater can indeed create a forum where imagination is not only conceived but also materialized through the participants' bodies.

Applied theater and trauma

The first question that comes to mind when working with refugees is to determine which kind of stories and narratives to work on. I follow this process when beginning every project with refugees. I ask: *Should I focus on the journey story or the traumatic experience in their home community that brought refugees here? Should I focus on their stories from here in the host community?* In the text *Applied Theater: Resettlement: Drama, Refugees, and Resilience* (2015, p. 5), the authors decided to focus their refugee participants on stories centered on their post-arrival lives while directly avoiding pre-arrival stories. Their decision to do so was purposeful. With too little experience in addressing trauma from a psychological perspective, they decided to use symbols and metaphors so that they could create a distance and emotional protection. Each facilitator must weigh his or her own comfort and preparedness for negotiating trauma and emotional distress. Those who are well trained in counseling, social work, or art therapy may be interested in staging exercises that tackle some of the sensitive issues surrounding pre-departure and journey stories. Those with more solidly theater or arts-practice backgrounds may find it more useful to work on host community and civic engagement issues.

When dealing with community members who have experienced trauma and who are still living in a transitional situation such as a refugee center or refugee camp, one must consider that the stories of their departure from their home country, journey, and arrival in the host location are their most valuable possessions. There are two kinds of stories that are dominant among the refugee narratives. One is the story of loss. It focuses on the way in which they had to leave their homes and move to their new host community. The other is the story of the beautiful past before the war. In this story, they reminisce about the positivity of life at home in a time before their current trauma.

These two narratives are polar in nature, and refugees will most likely develop one or the other while trying to find a way to balance their understanding of their "old selves" with the realities of their new lives. Most refugees leave their homelands with few or even no material belongings. They may have their passports (some do not even have those), the clothes they are wearing, and memory banks full of all kinds of stories. While they are traveling to their safe destination, they chart their traumatic narratives while living them. These traumas become the refugee's driving discourse. The particular narrative of their departure, however, can be the element required to jumpstart a new life in their host community.

Throughout the journey of displacement, refugees not only experience their own trials, but they also become witnesses for other people's hardships. For many, whether walking for miles through the lower Syrian desert or walking for days across the forests of Eastern Europe, the journey is done as a random collective of unrelated individuals. Each person becomes very attuned to what they see and hear, filtering a huge amount of information and images that they witness and keeping only what supports their own survival, necessarily dismissing that which may threaten their hope of reaching a place of safety and security. Another goal of the applied theater workshop may be to open possibilities for more stories to be discussed, both those belonging to the participants themselves and those they have seen, blocked, and need to process for full recovery.

While leading applied theater workshops with refugees, I try to capture the most intense moments of their stories: moments of despair, hope, bravery, etc., when a person was indeed in the middle of "it." While conducting this kind of work, I lean on research that connects applied theater with its therapeutic uses. Gurle (2018), for instance, writes about enhancing the awareness of emotions among Syrian refugees in Turkey. Jones (2015) also addresses trauma and drama therapy. In these two studies and others, there is a focus on how sharing of such a moment, re-telling it, embodying it, and reliving it can trigger an emotional response from the narrator and other workshop participants. To trigger such a response, the facilitator should work hard to break any power dynamics that might exist in the workshop so that everyone feels safe to explore their personal stories without being judged.

Power dynamic and hierarchy in applied theater

Breaking pre-established social hierarchies in an applied theater workshop is an essential step since the work is rooted into getting people to think together about a specific issue or challenge that they are facing. One important strategy that I use at the outset is to make clear that theater experience is not a prerequisite to enter the workshop. I do not sort the participants in my workshops based on whether they have any theater experiences, because some may while others may not, and disclosing that information could create a power dynamic between the participants that I try to avoid.

Equity in the workshop starts right from the beginning, as I always open my workshops with everyone standing in a circle. The circle for me is a metaphor for equality, and it even includes me as a facilitator. I, too, am part of the group. Each and every one in the workshop will have a say in the discussion/reflection or in creating the scenes. However, I am also keen on making every voice heard as part of the work relating to promoting the individual voice. The question is how to balance between nurturing the individual voice and creating the collective voice. While doing that, I keep the theory of public narrative in the back of my mind as I work.

There has to be a fine line between challenging the oppressive structure that is based on acquired knowledge and skills, such as education degrees, culture, and skills such as music or language and between acknowledging those structures. In my personal practice, I tend to acknowledge these skills and achievements on a personal level; challenging them should be done on a collective level. Sometimes, I acknowledge a participant's personal achievement during my reflection sessions, which happen sometimes individually with workshop participants. By separating these indicators of social, age, or gender status from the workshop activity, I am often able to equalize participants.

Practitioner reflection in applied theater

Most applied theater researchers such as Rohd (1998), Saxton, J., & Prendergast, M. (Eds.) (2009), Kandil, Y. (2016), Taylor (2003) lean on the use of the reflection phase and consider it an essential stage in applied theater work. Reflection in applied theater can happen on many occasions, and it can be a direct process conducted by the facilitator or it can be an indirect process that happens among the participants themselves.

A facilitator may even conduct a reflection session after each activity. In my own practice, I tend to lead these activities swiftly by asking very simple questions such as *What did this game or exercise do to you?* or *What kind of skills can you draw from practicing this exercise or game?*

The central idea is that reflection can and should happen all the time during the workshop. I sometimes hang flip charts on the wall and ask participants to quickly withdraw from the activity to write a word or a sentence that captures what they feel and then invite them to rejoin the exercise when they are done. Other times, I intentionally give the group a break when I feel the discussion is heated, and I do that because I sense as a facilitator that it might be productive at that point for that group to have the time to talk among themselves without the interference of the facilitator or the workshop setting.

Reflection is extremely important in applied theater because it allows participants to connect what is happening in the workshop to their daily lives. It also allows participants to broaden the way they look at their challenges. An experienced facilitator might shift her plans based on the participants' reflections and may know exactly when to capitalize on a specific moment during the reflection to open new possibilities within the process of the workshop.

As an academic practitioner, I also use research as my own reflection. While leading, documenting, writing, and reflecting on my workshops, I perceive the entire process as a continuum, a research practice that connects the dots among conceiving, executing, and writing. I construct the research as a narrative that not only carries my voice as a researcher, but also carries the voices of the participants, collaborators, and people who work at the refugee camps as well as the voices of the other scholars who precede me. Reflection also is a good way to channel the emotional processes that both the facilitator and participants have gone through.

Empathy in applied theater

A report on a recent project using theater of the oppressed as a tool to address Syrian refugee issues in Turkey found that using theater increased empathy and understanding (Alshughry, 2018). For me, empathy involves the ability to understand the current feelings of the other person. Not the past feelings but the current ones Kalisch (1973). Empathy in applied theater is a dialogical process that allows participants to more deeply connect with their own feelings, feelings that are otherwise overlooked, neglected, or ignored in light of the difficulties of day-to-day life.

In applied theater workshops, participants finally get the chance to practice what might be called "active listening." I define active listening by not only paying attention to all the details of the story that is being told, but also by empathizing with the person who is telling the story. Active listening also involves paying close attention to the flux of emotions that are surfacing. Eliciting empathy may pose a challenge to some, especially if the listener does not want to open up or he or she is resisting the reception of these emotions.

Surprisingly enough, I have found refugee communities to be some of the most empathetic. There is a special bond between displaced people, even if they have just met for the first time. Their shared experiences, however varied, have more or less the same patterns of life-threatening events, disposition, dislocation, applying for refugee status, and integration Karaoğlu, E. (2015). It is not only remarkable that patterns of their experiences are similar, but also that share a single concept that is always present, the concept of "loss."

When a participant begins sharing her story about the route she took in getting to Germany, as a facilitator, I do not need to give any instructions. The participants immediately engage with the storyteller in a way that I rarely see outside of this context. Their eyes and ears focus, and an emotional connection emerges so strong that you can almost hear the wheels of the brain churning while the listeners are creating analogies and drawing conclusions based on their own displacement stories. In one of the workshops, there was a young participant who was attending with his mother; he was a Syrian refugee who took the "death boat" from Turkey to Greece with his family. He was (by the way) the only one in the group who could speak German even though he had been in Germany for only 7 months.

That young child who was barely 9 years old told me, "Teacher, it is an experience that you cannot understand until you go through it." This humbling statement made me think again about my work with refugees and about all the planning and organizing that I do before and while leading an applied theater experience. It is a great amount of work, yet the minute a specific group circles around one shared story which touches on the instinctual desire of survival, the power of that story is released into the group; the power of a story that suddenly becomes both personal and communal can hold the key to the success of an entire applied theater workshop.

Applied theater facilitator

Sara Orr (2015) addresses the use of participatory theater as a tool to empower peers to build knowledge together. Empowerment in applied theater is a structural mechanism that should end in a concrete outcome in the form of a newly constructed mutual awareness. Orr claims that the facilitator's role is the most integral part of the applied theater process. Seemingly, the facilitator role can be seen as one dimensional and limited to leading games or exercises, but the complexity of the role is impeded in part because of the many hats facilitators must wear. One minute he is leading an exercise, and another he is part of it. One minute she is acting, and another she is directing. One minute they are leading a discussion, and another they are listening.

In addition to all of this, the facilitator must pay specific attention to the power dynamics of the participants (who is active, who is not, who is taking most of the air time, who is bored, who is excited, who is opening up, who is not, who is controlling the conversation, who is speaking less, etc.). The facilitator has to be the leader but one who delegates power to the other participants rather than a leader who controls the power. The facilitator has to add a sizable input of aesthetic value to the experience, but it should not be so much that participants begin thinking about the product and forget about their processes.

In other areas of this book, and especially in Chapter 3, I pay much more detail to the process of facilitation and the various considerations of the facilitator who is working with refugees. Those ideas are, for the most part, too elaborate to effectively summarize here. However, I wish to now and will continue to draw attention to the term *care* in consideration of the facilitator's role. This concept must be inherent in every element of the process, from conception to conclusion, and it must guide each decision a workshop leader makes.

On reaching a dead end

Even though I look forward to any new workshop I am assigned to lead, I find myself following the same organizational patterns with minor modifications: warm-up games, posing a question, frozen images, and then discussions. This roadmap can shift or be elaborated upon, depending upon the group dynamics. Having a fixed pattern might restrict my work artistically, but it gives me the freedom to better focus on the workshop content. Some of the major questions that applied theater artists struggle with in defining their work are: *Is it theater? Is it social practice? Should the focus be on the aesthetics?* and *Should the work focus on its community aspect?*

As a facilitator, I advocate that to embody the core ethics of applied theater we must move the focus of attention to the group and away from executing the facilitator's agenda. To accomplish this goal, facilitators must approach the work with an open mind and heart and use their facilitation tactics to sense where the group is focused and help them to achieve their potential. I recall here an example from my work with a group of Syrian refugee women in Jordan. The women did not show any interest in performing, nor in even playing theater games, but they were really interested in telling their stories and discussing them. I drew upon my arsenal of techniques to quickly change the focus of the workshop so that it matched the group's dynamic. I remember shifting right away to public narrative techniques which helps me to be attentive to the group's goal and yet allows participants to share their tales.

The question that came out of my work in that particular episode was how to create a distinction between the stories that were told in the workshop format and those stories that were told among the same women while they were talking by themselves. To create this distinction, I devised a structure that prioritized the details of the stories. I also recall focusing on aesthetics, which was helpful in distinguishing between the daily tale of the refugee and the meta-daily (workshop time and space) of the refugee. The aesthetics followed simple guidelines such as posing, breathing, and making sure there was an opening and a closure for each tale. Such techniques helped me as a facilitator to circumvent the dead end of the practice.

A personal theory of practice

I recall Ahmad, a Syrian refugee in Germany, who told me that Germany was implicated in what was happening in Syria. Turkish forces are there, French weapons are there, American soldiers are there, Iranians, Russians . . . and after all, everyone is blaming refugees for leaving Syria and running for their lives to Europe. The problem is not Syrians, Ahmad believed. From his perspective, the problem is the meddling in what is happening in Syria. Through this discussion, Ahmad was questioning my applied theater work with refugees. He was implying that my applied theater workshops are not able to end the refugee crisis, as it is only one simple solution for a problem that is so big.

I agree with Ahmad. I start this book by sharing that I do not have any illusions or utopian dreams that my work with refugees has permanently changed lives. My work at most has created moments of critical awareness, moments of empathy, and moments of solidarity or connection. Yet, I do believe that there is a tremendous amount of value in doing applied theater with refugees, even if change may not be imminent.

Ola Johansson (2010) states that community-based theater can offer a cultural and historical perspective of the challenges, yet it cannot offer a guaranteed way of achieving efficacy. In fighting HIV/AIDS, for example, a part of the battle would be to change personal behavior in order for the community as a whole to survive. Johansson states that such projects will still have limitations, even if we do many theater projects and they are all well attended. The HIV/AIDS epidemic will persist until issues of gender inequality and homophobia are openly confronted. Similar to Johansson's argument, I am not fooling myself by thinking that applied theater by itself would either end the refugee crisis or ensure the seamless integration of refugees into their host communities, but it takes us one step closer to addressing the traumatic experiences of refugees.

Like other marginalized groups, refugees often feel that they have been stripped of agency. They are unable to conceptualize that changing their personal behaviors can additionally create social change; however, to fully enact new lives in their host communities they must do just that. Each refugee's integration process will vary based on the city or country they live in. For example, in some cities in Germany, refugees can stay for up to a year in a refugee camp with limited mobility, unable to enroll in a language course until their case is settled. Refugees consciously aware of this dilemma are unable to begin effecting change in their lives. Thus, they are stripped of their sense of agency.

Applied theater is able to restore an individual's confidence, bringing their voice back to them, and in doing so restore their human dignity. Similar to Johansson, however, I believe that applied theater work with refugees has limitations. A workshop or a program might indeed restore some dignity to the refugee, but she will go back to her refugee center and be faced again with the ugly reality of her current life. For a change to occur, there must be a comprehensive approach to deal with refugee resettlement and more importantly with root causes of refugee crises. Without this level of conversation and meaningful collaboration between refugee communities and host communities, social programs of all kinds will remain ineffective at enacting widespread, meaningful social change.

References

Al-Krenawi, A. (2019). Living in a refugee camp: The Syrian case in Jordan. In *Culture, diversity and mental health – Enhancing clinical practice. Advances in mental health and addiction* (pp. 119–132). Cham: Springer. doi:10.1007/978-3-030-26437-6_7

Alshughry, U. (2018). Non-violent communication and theater of the oppressed: A case study with Syrian refugee women from the Kareemat Centre in Turkey. *Intervention, 16*(2), 170–174. doi:10.4103/INTV.INTV_45_18

28   *Theory, issues, and stories*

Balfour, M., Bundy, P., Burton, B., Dunn, J., & Woodrow, N. (2015). *Applied theater: Resettlement: Drama, refugees and resilience.* New York, NY: Bloomsbury Publishing.

Fiorella, L., & Mayer, R. E. (2015). *Learning as a generative activity: Eight learning strategies that promote understanding.* Cambridge: Cambridge University Press. doi:10.1017/CBO9781107707085

Fisher, A. S. (2005). Developing an ethics of practice in applied theater: Badiou and fidelity to the truth of the event. *Research in Drama Education: The Journal of Applied Theater and Performance, 10*(2), 247–252. doi:10.1080/135697805 00103992

Gurle, N. S. (2018). Enhancing the awareness of emotions through art and drama among crisis-affected Syrian refugee children in southeast Turkey. *Intervention, 16*(2), 164–169. doi:10.4103/INTV.INTV_41_18

Johansson, O. (2010). The limits of community-based theater: Performance and HIV prevention in Tanzania. *TDR, 54*(1), 59–75. Retrieved May 19, 2020, from www.jstor.org/stable/40650522

Jones, P. (2015). Trauma and dramatherapy: Dreams, play and the social construction of culture. *South African Theater Journal, 28*(1), 4–16. doi:10.1080/101375 48.2015.1011897

Kalisch, B. J. (1973). What is empathy? *The American Journal of Nursing, 73*(9), 1548–1552.

Kandil, Y. (2016). Personal stories in applied theater contexts: Redefining the blurred lines. *Research in Drama Education: The Journal of Applied Theater and Performance, 21*(2), 201–213. doi:10.1080/13569783.2016.1155408

Karaoğlu, E. (2015). *The role of social dominance orientation, empathy and perceived threat in predicting prejudice of Turkish citizens toward Syrian immigrants* (Master's thesis). German Institute for International and Security Affairs Middle East Technical University, Ankara, Turkey.

Orr, S. H. (2015). Training the peer facilitator: Using participatory theater to promote engagement in peer education. *Research in Drama Education: The Journal of Applied Theater and Performance, 20*(1), 110–116. doi:10.1080/13569783.20 14.983466

Prentki, T. (2015). *Applied theater: Development.* London: Bloomsbury Methuen Drama.

Rohd, M. (1998). *Theatre for community, conflict & dialogue: The hope is vital training manual.* Heinemann Drama.

Saxton, J., & Prendergast, M. (Eds.). (2009). *Applied theater: International case studies and challenges for practice.* Bristol, UK: Intellect Books.

Skeiker, F. F. (2011). Performing orphanage experience: Applied theater practice in a refugee camp in Jordan. *Applied Theater Researcher/IDEA Journal, 12*, 1–8.

Taylor, P. (2003). *Applied theatre: Creating transformative encounters in the community.* Heinemann Drama.

Thompson, J. (2005). *Digging up stories: Applied theater, performance and war.* Manchester: Manchester University Press.

Tiltnes, Å. A., Zhang, H., & Pedersen, J. (2019). The living conditions of Syrian refugees in Jordan- results from the 2017–2018 survey of Syrian refugees inside and outside camps. *Fafo Report*, 1–172. Retrieved from https://reliefweb.int/sites/reliefweb.int/files/resources/67914.pdf

United Nations High Commissioner for Refugees. (n.d.). *Syria emergency*. Retrieved April 12, 2020, from https://www.unhcr.org/en-us/syria-emergency.html

United Nations. (n.d.). *Syria emergency*. Retrieved from www.unhcr.org/en-us/syria-emergency.html

Wolf, S. (2007). On the gender continuum. In A. E. Armstrong & K. Juhl (Eds.), *Radical acts: Theater and feminist pedagogies of change* (pp. 171–179). San Francisco, CA: Aunt Lute Books.

2 Jordan

Youth, gender, and discovering the individual

When Tunisian activists and youth began peaceful demonstrations in 2010, later known as the Arab Spring, little could they have known that they would spark a cascade of political movements throughout the region. Since then, Tunisia has been moving slowly but steadily toward a democratic transformation. In other Arab states, even though the Arab Spring revolutions affected changes to political systems, they were unable to create political stability, which has resulted in both social and economic unrest. In Syria, Libya, and Yemen, the Arab Spring resulted in civil war. Even now as we bridge into the third decade of the new millennium, Syria and Libya are on the verge of division, and the crisis has produced a flux of millions of refugees from Syria, in particular.

According to the United Nations High Commissioner for Refugees' (UNHCR) Syria Regional Refugee Response statistics, as of January 2016, there were approximately 4.6 million registered refugees in countries neighboring Syria. That means that there are almost five million registered refugees in Jordan, Lebanon, Turkey, Iraq, and Egypt, in addition to approximately six million refugees displaced within Syria itself. These staggering numbers are the largest since World War II. Of the five million refugees in the region, 600,000 are registered in Jordan. Fifty percent of those refugees are women in vulnerable situations and in an extremely challenging economic context. Although the UNHCR has combined forces with international organizations, the Jordanian government, and local NGOs, their efforts have mostly fallen short of the social and emotional needs of this population.

Media coverage for diasporic identities

Despite the media coverage of the refugee crisis, the refugee as an individual is mostly perceived as existing with a blank identity, with others attempting to fill the void of this identity through contrived discourses. Generally speaking, there are two kinds of dominant discourses that shadow the refugee coverage in public opinion. The first one is what I call a *demonizing* discourse in which the refugee is portrayed as someone who is coming to the host community to take advantage of the social welfare system, to dictate his or her own agenda on the host community, and to disturb the fabric of the host community, not to mention the possible threat that a refugee poses to national security. The second discourse is purely humane, portraying the refugee as a complete innocent who cannot be anything but a good person. I argue that these two discourses have done harm to the plight of the refugee as both establish expectations of the refugee and regard him or her as representing the agendas of both discourses without paying attention to the complexities of each and every refugee's story.

Both discourses fail to fathom the refugee identity, which, similarly to any other identity, is in a constant state of development in relationship to society. As Hammack puts it, "the process of identity development represents the link between self and society," (2008, p. 224). It becomes difficult for refugees who are both living their trauma and being aware of the media discourse that is accompanying their journey to reconstruct an identity because it is troubled simultaneously by their own lived experience and echoed by a one-sided public portrayal. Applied theater during these times becomes an excellent tool to assist Syrian refugees navigating their identity transformation processes.

This chapter focuses on my applied theater practice with refugees in Jordan, with specific reference to two workshops I led there with Syrian refugee youth. The program aimed at empowering youth refugees at Zaatari Refugee Camp in the northern part of Jordan and in the Community Development Centre in Zarqa, a city that is 20 miles north of Amman.

These two workshops were part of a thematic series of workshops I led entitled "My Name, My Story," a conceptual framework based on applied theater work I began in Jordan when I felt that there had to be more done to connect newly diasporic Syrian refugees with their post-Syrian identities. My initiative had two major goals. The first goal was to use the process of sharing the stories of their names and creating personal narratives as a stepping stone to help participants create a social bond among themselves. The second goal was to empower the participants. Empowerment came naturally when participants felt their personal narratives were given time and attention and when they were able to create short, simple scenes during the workshop.

In the last hour of the workshop, the participants shared their personal narratives in an intimate setting, to which I invited their parents. Another way to empower the youth is by offering them a platform to showcase their talents. For example, a girl who taught herself to speak English while living in a tent in Zaatari Camp was given a chance in the workshop to express herself in English. A boy who taught himself some acrobatic movements was given a chance during the workshop to exhibit his skills, as well. In all of these episodes, I felt that applied theater had been a successful tool in bringing young people together and helping them share meaningful moments that pushed them to navigate questions of their identities.

Applied theater as a responsive tool for empowering post–Arab Spring refugees

Applied theater is broadly defined as the use of theater skills in non-theatrical spaces, with the aim to empower the individuals of a community, or to raise discussion on a specific social issue. Applied theater intersects with other concepts such as theater in education, theater for social change, theater for development, and social theater.

Most applied theater practices utilize the theater workshop format as a tool to communicate a message or spark a dialogue with participants. Personally, when working with the refugee community, my main goal is not to offer them a site for entertainment. Rather, as performance ethnographer Conquergood (1988, p. 180) explains it, I hope to foster "a playful creativity that will help them affirm their past identities as well as equip them with skills that will help them to adapt to their new environment." Within the applied theater workshop format, participants are encouraged to tell their stories, to process them, and to rationalize their personal discourses while historicizing their identities by means of sharing personal narratives.

Within my applied theater practice, I focus on navigating identity through the process of creating personal narratives. The connection of these stories to identity is crucial because "narratives create identity at all levels of human social life" (Loseke, 2007, p. 661). Developing the personal narrative can be an excellent tool with which participants may explore stories from the past, as these stories, whether constructed by the participants themselves or told and shared with others, will play an important role in defining their self-concept (Fivush, 1991). The personal narrative of a participant will be acted out and expressed in a physical manner through frozen-image techniques.

In my work, the personal narrative is further connected to the embodiment of the story. In that regard, identity expression includes verbal and physical activities. For example, after a participant tells her story, I ask her to find three physical movements that represent her identity, broadly speaking. Because of restrictions regarding the exhibition of the body, especially within an Arab context and more specifically when working with a participant who is wearing a hijab, for example, I ask that the movements be simple and subtle. Walking from point A to point B slowly and then sitting on a chair can be enough if the participant is aware that her walk is timed and if she is aware of all the muscles involved in these simple movements. The point is not to theatrically exhibit the body in a particular aesthetic or performative style, but rather to be aware of the potential of the body to support and enhance the expression of the personal narrative. Creating a physical awareness while constructing the personal narrative will open participants to an understanding of the development of their identities, and it also will allow participants to better contextualize their lives.

Within the context of refugees in Jordan, where the concept of identity is deeply rooted in the question of origin and connection to the nation state, the personal narrative sometimes turns out to be about answering the question, "Where am I from?" Personal identity is being supplanted within this community through the identification of someone's origin, in large part because this identifies one person in relationship to another. For example, when an international aid worker asks a refugee where he is from, he is most likely to answer that he is from Syria; however, when a fellow refugee asks him the same question, he is most likely to answer that he is from a specific town in Syria. Identity formation in this regard becomes a concept determined by the way a refugee would like to be identified in front of the "other."

The question of identity is of crucial importance in the Arab region. Although Arab states, as we know them in the Levant, were formed less than 100 years ago, the way Arabs perceive their relationship to their nation state is of vital importance. In that regard, the Jordanian is different from the Syrian, who is different from the Lebanese and the Egyptian. Despite the shared language, a predominantly Islamic culture, and geographic proximity, newly established Arab nation states have been mostly successful in building up nationhood apparatuses and developing their own distinctive identities.

Understanding these facts helps us understand that being a Syrian in Jordan is not an easy assimilation. Syrian refugees in Jordan continuously find themselves in situations in which they must contextualize their identities and negotiate their presence in Jordan. They are not Jordanians, although some of them have lived there since 2011. Herein a tension is created in the way they identify both ethnically and culturally; many will attempt to preserve their Syrianhood because they are unable to feel they belong in their new nation state of residence. All of this information must be weighed when preparing for applied theater work with Syrian refugees in Jordan. This information will not only dictate the content of the workshops, but it will also inform the choice of applied theater techniques that are to be used.

Within the context of my own applied theater work with Syrian refugees, I discovered that focusing on drafting monologues proved to be the most helpful and appropriate tool because most often the population derives from a conservative background, and participants have already established ideas that prevent them from using their bodies as tools for communicating ideas. Within this particular episode of my work, and while I could have used simple frozen-image techniques when appropriate, I have depended heavily on monologue work as a tool that defines my applied theater practice.

Monologue benefit while working on identities

Applied theater can be instrumental in assisting refugees, particularly as they attempt to integrate into new cultural contexts. I believe that using the personal monologue as an applied theater technique could be an excellent tool to navigate the split between the self and collective in a refugee setting. This form allows for the assertion of individuality and invites those who witness monologues devised by refugees to listen closely to the narrative. Theater scholar Snyder-Young (2011, p. 949) acknowledges the transformative power of the monologue to navigate traumatic situations, stating that the monologue form is an "act of redemption, a way of creating a sober identity in a recovery process, a celebration of survival, a method of educating housed audiences." Snyder-Young argues that personal monologues help to "construct [one's] identity as a survivor" (2011, p. 948). I find this description of the benefits of the monologue form while doing applied theater applicable, especially within the context of Syrian youth refugees in Jordan where almost each and every one of them is thinking of himself or herself as a victim and not as a survivor.

I have noticed during my work with Syrian refugees in Jordan that there is a general sense of self-deprecation that permeates the refugee community and is particularly problematic for youth refugees. I believe that applied theater and the adoption of the monologue form in this episode of their lives can aid in transforming that "victimized" feeling into a "survival" sentiment. The sense of victimhood among Syrian refugees in Jordan is the result of many factors, but primarily it derives from the perception of refugees within the host community. During my work in Zaatari Camp, there were two dominant discourses circling among Jordanians. The first narrative was fueled by anger because refugees were competing with the locals for the scarce resources allocated to towns in the northern part of Jordan that had been facing economic difficulties even before the refugee crisis. The other narrative was colored by pity wherein members of the host community ached for the refugees. These two polar narratives on refugees affect the well-being of the refugees themselves and contribute to the perpetuation of their victimhood. With this in mind, I entered applied theater workshops with the sole purpose to transform their "victimhood" to "survivalhood."

I also use applied theater workshops as qualitative research sites that allow me to better understand the refugee experience, and simultaneously to empower the refugees themselves. While in the field, I am informed by qualitative methods that depend on extensive interviews combined with observation which allow the investigator to understand the structure and development of his subject's personhood and motivations. However I may appropriate these methods in the practice of applied theater, I have also developed my own adaptations of qualitative research. For example, I replace the interview phase with a collective theater performance that I use as a hook to invite participants to tell their stories and perform them so that *they* can better understand the structure and development of their identities. This and other ways are examples of how applied theater practitioners can utilize the methods of seasoned qualitative researchers to accomplish the goals of intellectual advancement and individual empowerment simultaneously.

While this chapter is limited in that it focuses on only two workshops with small numbers of participants, and it thereby risks that the conclusions drawn may not be based on representative samples, the main focus is not to understand the way in which a youth refugee is grappling with a changing identity but rather to create a method or a mode that can be helpful for other social workers and theater artists to adopt while working with youth refugees in the Middle East. Having said that, it should be noted that this module is based on having a facilitator who comes from the same background as the community with which he is working. In this case, I present myself as a Syrian facilitator who is working with a group of Syrians. This particularity of my own identity adds another level of consideration, especially when working with fellow Syrian refugees.

My decision to work with refugees presented a personal challenge in the way I would be perceived while leading the workshops; being Syrian myself could have both pros and cons. While having an applied theater facilitator who shares the language and culture of the participants will encourage them to open up and to feel safe, there is still heated political debate among Syrians about adherence to or rejection of the current regime. Participants might be concerned that the facilitator has a political agenda that does not match theirs. The Arab Spring has generated increased controversy among activists, scholars, and the general public. This controversy is created in part by the discontented segments of the population and elites, with instability caused by the Arab Spring (Korotayev, Issaev, Malkov, & Shishkina, 2014). Citizens in the Arab region have been divided according to whether they side *with* or *against* the Arab Spring. The division has been evident even in linguistic discourse. For example, the term "revolution" is used by those who support the Arab Spring, whereas those who support the various governments refuse to use this term.

I have faced this controversy while both practicing and describing my work. When I describe the refugees' challenges as an outcome of the political and humanitarian crisis, I get criticism from activists in the opposition who insist on addressing the refugees' issues as an outcome of the brutality of the government. Terminology has had an impact on my work with these refugees, as using a word that one group opposes will create an unsafe environment and prevent participants from feeling secure enough to share their thoughts.

An interesting example regarding the terminology conflict and how it can affect my work with Syrian refugees starts with the word that describes the political unrest in Syria. Should I call it a "revolution"? If I do, then I am excluding refugees who might side with the regime. Or, should I call it a "crisis"? If I do that, then will I get backlash from refugees who side with the opposition? Therefore, I have tried my best to use neutral language in my workshops, and I avoid expressing my own political ideas. This encourages participants to feel secure when expressing their views, even if these ideas conflict with mine. My goal in the workshops has never been to create a unifying opinion about an issue but rather to highlight differences in the way that citizens are responding to a public event, and to create connections among the different views of participants.

With this spirit, focused on the humanitarian, and by detaching myself from the political – which in itself is a choice that can be interpreted as political – my goal in leading applied theater workshops in Jordan was to equip participants with simple performance skills that will help them to better express themselves within and beyond the workshop space. For example, in a session I led with young, all-female Syrian refugees in Zarqa, and right after the warm-up games, I talked about the importance of stories in shaping our visions, and I told the story of my name. In this example, I shared the meaning of my name and the way in which the meaning of the name is connected to my own personality. I told the story of how my parents came to name me, and I explained the social and cultural connotations of my name. I told interesting stories related to my name, and then I used the story of my name as an excuse to talk about my life: my past, present, and future.

After demonstrating the story of my name, I divided the participants into small groups. Each group member then told the story of her name to her group. Then we began to act out the stories. My methodology worked out well, as participants were able to move from the personal to the public and from the story to the theory. For example, Hiba was 23 years old when she participated in my workshop. She moved to Jordan in 2015, but before that she attended Damascus University, studied early-childhood education, and was prepared to work as a kindergarten teacher.

On her path to Zarqa, Hiba walked her way through the southern Syrian city of Daraa, crossed the border, and made her way to Zaatari Camp. After living in the camp for a couple of months, she was able to move out with the aid of a family connection During the time of the workshop, she was living in Zarqa, a conservative city in Jordan with a majority of low-income inhabitants. At the time Hiba participated in the workshop, she was still on the lookout for a job. Here is her story:

> My name is Hiba, I am named by my brother, and I have no prob-
> lem with my name. I like it. I never connected the link between the
> name and the life of a person, but when I came to Jordan, many things
> changed, and one of the things that changed is the way I perceive my
> name. I started to pay attention to the meaning of my name, which
> means giving without waiting to receive. I started to help in whatever
> capacity I can the people around me without asking to be paid back.
> Leaving Syria was not only leaving a home country, it was also leaving
> big dreams behind, a whole life. Now in Jordan, I am looking for a new
> place to belong to, maybe a new home. My name means home.

The workshop worked out well for Hiba, in that she explicitly noted that it allowed her to go back to the meaning of her name and connect its mean-ing to a trait in her personality: her desire to help others. The meaning of her name literally translates to "a gift" as she understands it and connects to her desire and willingness to help others. She said that she cannot help anyone financially; however, she can help with "good word," which translates to being positive. After connecting the meaning of her name to her personality, she moved right away to talk about her connection to her homeland, Syria. She is a person who tries her best to help Syrians and is being positive in the way she interacts with them. Hiba then moves from analyzing her name from a personality trait to making it a metaphor that will historicize her being, as this is the only continuous line in her journey.

Names as a cultural starting point and safe common ground for story-sharing with young Arab refugees

It is challenging to get youth who participate in applied theater workshops to open up and share their personal narratives, especially since such work-shops are often limited to a short time frame. I recall here a workshop I led in Zaatari Camp where I was limited to only two sessions of five hours each. This limited time is not unusual within applied theater workshops in the Middle East. To make the best out of the short time frame, I decided to be selective. Instead of asking participants to share their entire life stories, I decided to ask them to tell me the stories of their names. Sharing the story of one's name is a normative cultural practice within Arab communities; hence, every name could either have a meaning or could evoke a cultural connotation. Names can be an indicator of urban or rural ties: the name "Bana" is most likely to be given to a girl who lives in a city, while the name "H'neea" is often given to a girl who is tied to a rural community. Moreover, names can offer strong indicators of religious affiliations, which is relevant in Arab states where religion is an important issue. As an example, "Mohammad" is a Muslim name, while "Botros" is a Christian name.

Most importantly, almost every name in Arabic has a meaning: "Haadia" means "calm person," "Hibba" means "gift," etc. An analysis of the meaning of names in connection to their current life situations was an excellent starting point to invite participants to open up. For example, I can ask Haadia, "Do you feel you are really calm? Or is it just your name? Do you remember specific moments in your life where you felt you were really calm? Would you like to share?" The name monologue exercise will bring youth refugees back to their identities, and it will allow them to create a link between their current refugee identity and their pre-displacement identities.

While working with youth refugees, especially during a workshop like the one I just described in Zarqa, I prepare with the knowledge that participants are occupied most of the day with the hardships of their daily lives, of getting food coupons, keeping themselves warm, or finding a way to shower. Living with such hardship causes even young people to think less about themselves. They have had to put aside their hopes and aspirations, their thoughts about home, the lives they once had, and even the life that awaits them in unpredictable and unscripted futures. Given the weight of these psychological burdens, it is difficult for them to reflect on and process what is happening in the now.

Creating personal narratives within an applied theater workshop becomes an excuse for participants to tell stories related to their own lives in the past, present, and future, and to compare stories from their past with those from their present in the camp. They note the changes and transformations within themselves and the way they want to be remembered in the future. Narratives focused on the most personal aspect of the individual – his or her name – help historicize the timeline of their lives and bring them back to themselves, more specifically, to their individual identities, which are being affected by their challenging circumstances, social traditions, and community pressures Gregg (207). This process will help them to reconstruct, remember, and rebuild their identities. Sharing the personal narrative becomes a channel for the young women to build a new awareness about themselves as

individuals and in relationship to the community, and building this awareness is the first step of empowerment.

Isolating the individual narrative

Syrian refugees attempting to negotiate the disconnect between their lived
experience and that narrative framed in media coverage will experience an
added psychological burden, hindering their recovery from the traumas of
displacement and the formation of a new post-displacement identity.

While narrative and identity are conceptualized as key elements in repro-
ducing the political conflict, Philip Hammack (2010) argues in his study
of refugee narratives that to the local community integrating refugees is
a practice of both "benefit" and "burden," beneficial in its ability to serve
as a tool for personal and social change and burden as integrating refugees
requires economic, social change as well as identity transformation on the
part of the host community. Syrian refugees, in particular, are fed with a
media narrative that portrays massacres and casualties in terms of number.
Certainly, the media will also show some individual images, but most of the
time the personal narratives of refugees are presented in fragments and are
not representative of the full story.

Since before fleeing their homes and throughout their journeys to an
interim or final destination, refugee youth are shown these images depict-
ing their lives at every stage of the displacement process. Upon becoming
refugees, these youth join a collective global refugee narrative, one they
have seen played out for millions of others in the news and on social media.
Their experience of dislocation, therefore, is not individualized. There is
no personal refugee narrative. Rather, their stories too become part of the
generalized media discourse. At the point of arrival at an interim camp (e.g.
Zaatari Camp) or final destination (e.g. an apartment in Zarqua or perhaps
in West Jordan), membership in the collective can be beneficial for young
people while they are getting settled in the camp. However, in this space
their collective identity may supersede their personal identity.

Exactly at this point, applied theater becomes one of the sites where they
can reclaim their personal narratives. Applied theater becomes a site where
they can safely negotiate the reconstruction of their identity in connection
to their new surroundings.

More specifically, youth who had been living in Syria before the war
undergo a process of identity reformation, all while facing life-threatening
obstacles. After their deadly pilgrimage to Zaatari Camp, most of these
youths are now, while in the camp, getting used to what it means to live in
an actual tent in the middle of the desert.

Most Syrian refugees in Jordan come from the southern part of Syria where tribal connections and family affiliations are of importance. In Syria, each family would have lived in a small town where uncles, aunts, and extended family members are also their neighbors. Zaatari Camp, with its loose family connection, is their new home. I argue that this change in lifestyle adds to the trauma refugees suffer and negatively affects their psychological well-being. Therefore working on their psychological well-being is as important as working on providing them with food and water.

Hanan is one example of a refugee youth who benefited from the development and presentation of a personal narrative, namely the "Story of My Name" exercise. I met 19-year-old Hanan while leading a workshop in Zaatari Camp. Hanan was lucky to be able to go to school, but before starting school she had been displaced for one year, living in hiding with her family, who belong to one of the opposition groups in the southern part of Syria. Hanan witnessed a number of atrocities targeted at her family and held in her mind the dream of being able to share her family's stories by becoming a journalist.

Hanan shared that her name means "compassion." One of the problems that she faced when moving to the camp was the change of school curriculum because she came from Syria to Jordan where the curricula are different. While Hanan was struggling with school, she encountered another problem – electricity. Zaatari suffers from constant power shortages, and the fact that she was the oldest child in the house meant she had many chores to do. In the camp, her family shared a kitchen and bathroom with another family, and they had problems getting water to drink. They did not envision any opportunities on the horizon to improve their lives, and yet, everyone around kept telling them that they were lucky to be out of Syria and living in Jordan. Hanan struggled with this assumption. She wondered if it meant that they were lucky that no one was killing them. In the face of waiting in long lines for hours just to access drinking water, this "luck" seemed ironic to her.

Even though Hanan started with explaining the meaning of her name and her challenges, she moved right away to her aspiration of being a journalist. Hanan was very much aware of the false coverage of life in Zaatari Camp and began to see a future life in journalism as a way to share not only her family's story, but also those of the thousands of families struggling to survive in Zaatari. She was also able to make distinctions between the suggestions that refugees are lucky to have escaped Syria or that their lives are improved. Identifying and elaborating on these distinctions was essential for Hanan in developing her sense of self as an individual, separate from media depictions.

Diasporic identities and gender

Within their predominantly conservative home communities in Syria, I assume that the cultural identities of soon-to-be refugee youth were settled, as each one of them was a dependent person within the context of a collective culture. The trauma that they endured often appears to have transformed them, propelling them into the self-expression indicative of independent people in individualist cultures. The ramifications of this change should not be undermined as it will show on different social levels. For example, I personally noticed a new social paradigm emerging in terms of gender relationships during one of the workshops I led in Zaatari Camp.

In one of the workshops I led in Zaatari Camp, an Action Aid representative and I (Action Aid sponsored that workshop) were pleasantly surprised to see a mixed group of youth, both females and males, show up to participate. After they introduced themselves, I laid out the rules of the workshop, at which time I stressed that all of the participants' opinions were equal, and that the workshop was a judgement-free space. Right after I finished, one of the male participants interrupted the workshop and asked me to talk privately. I recall him telling me, "I am so sorry but I have to withdraw from the workshop. I am not comfortable to be in the same place with girls. When I signed up, I thought it would be an all-male workshop."

I sensed that the young man's decision to leave the workshop was a protest against depriving him of his superior status as a male in a patriarchal community and in reaction to the rules I had laid out clearly at the beginning of the workshop: that everyone is equal during the workshop time. The workshop allowed female participants like Nora, for example, to build up her narrative and be able, maybe for the first time since arriving in Zaatari, not only to voice herself but also enact her story as she wished. Nora decided to create her monologue with other workshop participants who acted out parts of her narrative.

Nora was 20 years old, with sparkling eyes. She finished high school, but her family was too poor to send her to university. While in Syria, she helped her family in peasantry work and by caring for her younger siblings. During that time and before seeking refuge in Jordan, Nora was immersed in watching films, primarily on the free MBC channels in the Arab world that show American films with Arabic subtitles almost around the clock. The films allowed Nora to travel in her mind because she could not travel in real life. In her monologue, she said:

> I would like to travel but my passion for travelling faces many challenges; one of them is the passport. At this point, I can't get a passport because I am a refugee, and even if I get a passport, my family will

object to my desire to travel because I am a girl. Another passion of mine is to learn how to do acrobat movements. An acrobat company came to the camp and was giving classes but I could not take the classes because I am a girl. As you can see, I cannot achieve these two dreams, but I am happy to be in a theater workshop, and maybe I can be an actress.

It was interesting that Nora did not start her story with the meaning of her name, even though the prompt of the workshop was to tell that story. She immediately began to talk about her life in the camp and about obstacles that she faced, starting with her passport. Hers is a classic refugee story because she was not allowed to have a passport issued to her while she was residing in Zaatari. Her dream of being an acrobat posed another challenge for her. She was not allowed to do it because it would require a type of bodily exposure and movement that is not accepted within her community. Body restriction is not required of boys, who are free to move about and exhibit their bodies publicly. Nora's desire to be an actress can be interpreted as a metaphor for her deep wish to play different social roles – the role of a traveler, an acrobat, and many more.

Technically, and unlike other stories from workshop participants, Nora shifted between narrating and enacting her story. She used other participants in the workshop to embody what was in her imagination. For instance, while she told how she was denied the opportunity to get a passport, one of the participants played the role of the officer who denied her the passport, and another female participant played Nora's role in applying for the passport. The character of Nora was not involved when she talked about her desire to be an acrobat. She used a male participant who is already involved in taking acrobatic classes in the refugee camp to embody her narration, while she talked about watching people take acrobatic classes. It was extremely important that Nora's story be narrated by her in her own voice and enacted by male participants who in their lives outside the workshop environment embodied the physicality that Nora desired. I believe that this is an important step toward gaining allies for young Arab women and allowing young male figures in the camp to sit, listen, and empathize with the suffering of a female youth refugee.

Nora was very much aware not only of restrictions put on her as a refugee, but also of restrictions put on her as a woman. Still she dreamed, and she seemed to be positive in finding a way to articulate her dreams and ambitions. These dreams and ambitions are shared among other female refugees, but they are faced with the harsh realities in which they live. Nora's story aligns with what Jan Cohen-Cruz (2006, p. 103) addresses when she states, "The political potential of personal story is grounded not in particular subject matter but rather in storytelling's capacity to position even the least powerful individual in the proactive, subject position." The most powerful elements of my applied theater workshops in Jordan were the young Syrian women who struggled to find their voices and who were deprived of any opportunity to have a say in the way their lives were heading.

Identities and cultural trauma

Syrians, as a global ethnic and cultural collective, are experiencing what Jeffrey Alexander (2004, p. 1) calls "cultural trauma," which he explains "occurs when members of a collectivity feel they have been subjected to a horrendous event that leaves indelible marks upon their group conscious-ness, marking their memories forever and changing their future identity in fundamental and irrevocable ways."

Post-2011, Syrians are continuously constructing and naming a collective cultural trauma. The construction is active, as the trauma is ongoing. It is, therefore, still too early to talk about memory. Syrian refugees are still liv-ing the experience. Syrian refugees are treading water within their trauma, with no time to reflect on it. I argue that work needs to be done on the social and psychological levels to enable Syrian refugees to make sense of their traumatic experiences. Doing so will help foster a stronger shared identity that will give insights into how to end this trauma.

There is a sense among most of the refugees I have talked with, young and elderly, that there is nothing they could have done or can do to stop the war. While I share the same feeling of helplessness, I still find time to optimisti-cally practice my applied theater workshops so that those who have had to flee with only that which they could carry will be reminded of their bravery. They showed agency when they fled a war zone, and their agency was evident when they defied the fear of being killed during their journey to their host community. The minute they arrived at Zaatari Camp they abandoned their agency and were surrounded by bitter reality. But through extensive work on their psychological well-being, refugees, through applied theater and other forms of therapy in the arts or in traditional settings, may begin to heal. The ground will be set to restore the collective memory after the war ends.

Finale

While I feel humbled that I was able to lead these workshops with refugees, and while I feel so honored that youth in both workshops felt safe to share their stories and hopes with me, I left the work with many questions:

- How effective, really, is my work with young people?
- How can NGOs and governments find a balance between providing for the basic needs of refugees, such as food, clothing, shelter, etc., and addressing their psychological well-being?

- How do we gauge the efficacy of these workshops?
- To what extent did change really happen in the lives of the participants because of these workshops?
- How do I move forward in refining my work?
- What are the next steps needed to assist these communities?

Even though I do not have concrete answers for these questions, I can tell you this: if we want refugee youth to be able to articulate their hopes and dreams, we need to provide them with workshops that will give them opportunities to reflect on their identities and to be themselves. If we want a young woman such as Hiba to find a new, safe home, Hiba needs to be able to tell her story again and again. If we want Nora to achieve her dream and become an actress, she needs help while she is struggling in Zaatari Camp. She cannot achieve her dream if she is left alone. If we want Hanan to be a journalist, we need to make sure that she is able to go to school. If we want to share the stories of Hiba, Nora, and Hanan, we need applied theater to provide a venue where their voices will be heard. And finally, if we hope to counter the ugly atrocities of war, we must empower people to lift their voices.

References

Alexander, J. C. (2004). Toward a theory of cultural trauma. In B. Giesen, N. J. Smelser, P. Sztompka, J. C. Alexander, & R. Eyerman (Eds.), *Cultural trauma and collective identity* (pp. 1–30). Berkeley, CA: University of California Press.

Cohen-Cruz, J. (2006). Redefining the private: From personal storytelling to political act. In J. Cohen-Cruz & M. Schutzman (Eds.), *A Boal companion: Dialogues on theater & cultural practices* (pp. 103–111). London: Routledge.

Conquergood, D. (1988). Health theater in a Hmong refugee camp: Performance, communication, and culture. *TDR, 32*(3), 174–208. doi:10.2307/1145914

Fivush, R. (1991). The social construction of personal narratives. *Merrill-Palmer Quarterly, 37*(1), 59–81.

Gregg, G. S. (2007). *Culture and identity in a Muslim society (culture, cognition, and behavior)*. Oxford: Oxford University Press.

Hammack, P. L. (2008). Narrative and the cultural psychology of identity. *Personality and Social Psychology Review, 12*(3), 22–247. doi:10.1177/1088868308316892

Hammack, P. L. (2010). Identity as burden or benefit? Youth, historical narrative, and the legacy of political conflict. *Human Development, 53*(4), 173–201. doi:10.1159/000320045

Korotayev, A. V., Issaev, L. M., Malkov, S. Y., & Shishkina, A. R. (2014). The Arab Spring: A quantitative analysis. *Arab Studies Quarterly, 36*(2), 149–169. doi:10.13169/arabstudquar.2.2.0149

Loseke, D. R. (2007). The study of identity as cultural, institutional, organizational, and personal narratives: Theoretical and empirical integrations. *The Sociological Quarterly, 48*(4), 661–688.

Snyder-Young, D. (2011). Rehearsals for revolution? Theater of the oppressed, dominant discourses, and democratic tensions. *Research in Drama Education: The Journal of Applied Theater and Performance, 16*(1), 24–45. doi:10.1080/13 569783.2011.541600

3 Germany
Organizing and facilitating a workshop

Introduction

After years of studying, practicing, and teaching theater arts, I have come to the conclusion that to make a real change in the community, applied theater has to be practiced alongside – not behind or adjacent to – aesthetic theater. As a theater artist whose engagement has focused on using theater as a tool to address social issues, I came to this conclusion after practicing both applied and aesthetic theater and after witnessing the empowerment that an applied theater experience can transfer to its participants. For several years, most of my own theater practice has been spent running applied theater workshops. By trial and error, I developed techniques for every step from proposing a workshop to organizing and negotiating its parameters, recruiting participants, and then conducting the actual workshop.

Of the many types of applied theater techniques, I center the workshops on participants' stories, though not in the sense of storytelling performed for children or a dramatic monologue, but rather of using a story as a catalyst to encourage the participant to reflect on his or her life. Still, in these workshops participants narrate, so language is a crucial factor. Having said that, I prefer to utilize body narration, which is when I ask participants to create a parallel narration with their bodies that accompanies their linguistic narratives. My workshop design draws from several influences: many physical exercises are borrowed from the late Brazilian practitioner Augusto Boal (2013) and his Theater of the Oppressed method; I also use some techniques from the American practitioner/scholar Michael Rohd (1998), especially from his exercises that encourage participants to share their stories; and while working with immigrants and refugees, I use the work of Cécile Rousseau and others (2004) as a reference point, as she offers a vision of drama therapy that helps newly arrived immigrants and refugees adjust to the unfamiliar culture and avoid emotional repercussions of alienation and frustration.

This overall approach, from planning and preparing to facilitating the workshop, is flexible. While I repeat many of the steps across different sites and different groups, still, I am always improvising some aspects on the spot, adjusting some details. As other applied theater practitioners experience, while much of this process is planned, the actual steps almost never happen exactly as we anticipate. For example, while making the initial contact with the organization, one might discover that one organization is not interested. Perhaps another organization is interested but cannot find a suitable room to lead the workshop. When the workshop starts, one finds fewer or more people than were signed up, etc. So the approach to conducting a workshop can be seen as a series of questions, one at each juncture of the process: *Which space can I book for the event? Will I work with a group of all women, all men, or mixed? What warm-up seems best for this group?* And so on. Normally, I answer these questions intuitively, on the spot, and do not dwell much on them unless the situation calls for a more drastic adjustment.

My goal here is to articulate these moments of adjusting and deciding at each step of the process through the example of one workshop: a six-hour workshop in a refugee reception center in Hamburg, Germany (a temporary residence and kind of community center), with nine adult men, that – after warm-up and intermediary exercises – centered on them narrating and stylizing the stories of their journey experiences.

In 2015, I went to Germany to participate in a seminar entitled "Spirals of Dialogue." The seminar was hosted by Hamburg University and convened by Professor Gordon Michelle and his graduate students. Knowing that Germany, like other EU countries, was receiving thousands of refugees, I decided to run a workshop for refugees outside of the university. This brought me into a partly familiar situation: I would be working again with predominantly Arab participants, but they were not in Jordan or another Arab context, and they were not *only* Arabs. As refugees, they were minorities in Europe, not speaking the dominant language; they were people who had invariably suffered ordeals recently in their journeys to Germany; and they were transient, not yet integrated in regular neighborhoods, work, or school, and not at all certain of what their futures would look like.

First, to understand the context of the workshop, it helps to remember the larger view of refugees in Germany. According to the United Nations High Commissioner for Refugees (UNHCR), about one million refugees entered the EU zone in 2015 (Spindler, 2015). Under Chancellor Angela Merkel, Germany established an open-door policy, which enticed the highest number of refugees among the European states. The country has faced the challenges of accommodating them, providing shelter and food, "vetting" them (establishing that they pose no danger, deciding who deserves to be granted asylum), and eventually locating refugees in neighborhoods where they would begin to work or study. That first phase is slow. Their movement is restricted, and because most of them are not allowed to take German-language courses they are not able to interact much with locals or pursue an educational path. Adults cannot work formally. Residents in the reception center spend their days *waiting*. Before reaching this phase of waiting, moreover, all of them experienced difficult ordeals in their home-lands (the reasons pushing them to leave), and then on the journey to Germany. Each of these represents a trauma that may affect them in the present. Hence, they experience complex feelings yet have no productive activity or sign of advancement ahead. I hoped that the workshop could provide an example for the reception center of a creative way to engage the residents, one that also enables them to express their difficult experiences of migration to Germany.

First act: the trainer and the community

Arranging an applied theater workshop is not usually a straightforward process; it can take several steps, multiple phone calls, and a few visits to meet with staff at sites before finally locating a willing organization. Although the process is frustrating, it is informative. I have learned about the culture of specific organizations, bureaucratic processes, and the issues of the groups with which I work. In my ongoing work in Jordan between 2010 and 2015, I had mostly figured out the best protocols for arranging a workshop, but in this instance, I was new to the city and country and did not know the flow charts or cultural style of its government agencies and organizations. Before traveling there, I contacted one of the graduate students at Hamburg University whom I knew about with regard to her volunteering with specifically Arab-speaking refugees or asylum seekers. I sent her a project proposal and asked her to contact one of the refugee centers on my behalf.

One of the anchors of my method of applied theater is an assistant. The questions in locating someone had been: *Who would best assist me?* and *Who would be willing to help?* I always try to recruit someone local who knows the host organization and understands the community from which I will recruit participants. I usually try to identify an assistant who is a gender different from mine, assuming that there may be female participants in the workshop who would feel more comfortable if an assistant or co-facilitator is a woman. I am usually not keen on having an assistant who is a theater artist. I hold higher value for their work in social service and their ties to the culture of the community, assuming that the assistant has an interest in the arts in general and is someone who believes in the role of creating positive effects in the lives of the community members.

I had known the graduate student whom I recruited to assist me in that particular capacity from my time in Jordan, as she approached me in the past to help her set up a workshop to use theater as a tool for cultural dialogue between German and Jordanian youths. She was working on her Ph.D. in religious dialogue through the arts at Hamburg University. Even though her name (here, I will call her Khadija) gives the impression that she is of Arab origin, she is actually a white woman born to family that is Muslim and who knows Arabic well. Having an assistant in an applied theater workshop is something that has to be thought about carefully while planning. Assistants who share the same language and cultural references as the participants would be beneficial because they will serve as a bridge between the participants and the facilitator. In that capacity, they would allow the participants to feel more comfortable. On the other hand, having assistants who are not from the community would offer a different perspective and a view from the bridge that would help to see the work in context. In this particular case, Khadija was the kind of assistant who represented both sides of the coin. She shared the Islamic culture of the participants as she is Muslim, but at the same time, she is German. Khadija was the kind of assistant who could connect closely but also view from the bridge when needed. Most importantly, Khadija was extremely important in putting me in contact with German refugee centers. The fact that she speaks German and was able to communicate directly with the staff in the refugee center was essential for materializing this workshop.

Upon landing in Hamburg, Khadija informed me that after contacting the reception center she usually collaborated with, she was informed only one day before I arrived that we could not lead the workshop because the refugee center had been flooded with 200 new arrivals, and it was impossible for them to host us. The response reminded me of the actual grave realities of refugees. While getting lost in the logistics of organizing a workshop, sometimes a facilitator will overlook basic facts and questions related, for example, to how soon to approach refugees. Let's imagine that these 200 refugees have just arrived from Syria after crossing the sea to Greece and then walking their way across Europe to reach their destination. The walk through Europe might take anywhere from two weeks to two months and entail its own physical and psychological tolls. When would be the most appropriate time to start an applied theater workshop with them? What would be more urgent in their case? A theater workshop or basic volunteering? Food? Water?

I had to think of an alternative plan, and I was determined to lead a workshop while I was in Hamburg. Therefore, directly after she retrieved me from the airport, I requested that Khadija take me to one of the other refugee centers to ask about the possibility of leading a workshop there. While initially Khadija did not feel comfortable paying a visit without an appointment, she agreed to try it out. We stopped by the first refugee center and asked the security officer there if we could talk with the social activities organizer. The first center told us that it was impossible to lead a workshop at their facility on such a short notice, but they gave us a phone number for another center that might be open to the idea.

When Khadija called the suggested center, Fluchtlingsunterkunft, that is located in the northern part of Hamburg, they invited us to meet their management team. The center consisted of a couple of housing units, each one with two floors. The ground-floor housing held families, and the first-floor housing was for single men. The exterior was brightly painted, with a play area for the children. It was located conveniently in the city, close to public transportation. When I asked about the demographics of the people living around the center, I was told they were mostly retired people. As documented by Sophie Hinger in *Asylum in Germany: The Making of the "Crisis" and the Role of Civil Society* (2016), this model of housing for newly arrived refugees until they receive their formal refugee status seemed to be the norm in most German cities.

The administrators in this center were extremely welcoming and appreciative of the effort required to lead an activity with the refugees. Kathleen Gallagher (2015) advocates for theater to be a tool to awaken public officials about specific issues that a community is going through, and I found myself there in a simple encounter with center officials, triggering an interest in applied theater and its importance. They even seemed understanding of the importance of the role of the arts while working with refugee communities. I recall one of them telling me that she had been introduced to applied arts practice in the past, and she had always been on the lookout for such an opportunity that would help the refugees at the center. The initial conversation with them took place in German, and Khadija served as a translator. Right away, we signed the paperwork required for volunteers.

One of the questions involved in organizing workshops with refugees is the issue of language: should I lead the workshop in Arabic or in English? Leading the workshop in German was not an option in this case because I do not speak German, and the refugees themselves do not speak German. As I have already mentioned, refugees usually are not permitted to enroll in a German-language course while they are at the center. Volunteers do try to come and teach some German-language lessons, but it is not a consistent effort and tends to be done informally, which make the lessons ineffective most of the time. The only language-learning exception is for children who can register in a German course even while they are at the center. These conditions left me with the option either to lead the workshop in Arabic since I might have a group of Arab speakers, or in English in case I were to find out that those who signed up for the workshop were a combination of Arabs and other nationalities such as Iranians or Afghanis.

That decision affected the early steps, even before the workshop started, as I had to choose whether the design of our flyers to recruit participants would be in Arabic or in English. Deciding to write the flyer or to lead the workshop in Arabic in advance was not an option, as explained by the workers at the center. Had either been done in Arabic, it would have appeared as if the center were making an effort to welcome refugees from Arab-speaking countries, which would only have contributed to the division that already existed among refugee communities. At that time, it was common for non-Arabs to feel that Syrians were being treated preferentially. There was controversy and sometimes clashes between asylum seekers of Arab origin and those of other races, namely non-Arab Africans, as they saw themselves as competing for scarce resources and services. Syrians in particular have been treated as priority asylum seekers, which means their paperwork processes are expedited, and they get more attention from NGOs and aid workers. Deciding to restrict the workshop to Arab speakers would have created additional tension between Arabs and non-Arabs at the reception center. For this reason, the staff at the center advised us to make signs in both Arabic and English to recruit workshop participants.

When leading an applied theater workshop, it is also extremely important that the participants come willingly, which requires some social connection between the workshop trainers and the community. As an outsider, I was unknown to this community, and therefore the refugees would understandably feel cautious about my real intentions or how I might use their stories. Having Khadija, who was known to some members of the community, on my side was a guarantee that I would be trusted as a trainer. Khadija was an avid volunteer, and while we walked through the reception center, she was recognized by people who expressed their desire to be in the workshop because she would be in it.

While hanging the flyers before the workshop, we encountered some potential participants who reminded me that refugees are often very eager to describe their difficult journeys and present troubles in the host country. Khadija introduced me to a Syrian husband and wife who lived there, and we asked for their help in recruiting participants. They were extremely welcoming, happy to see Khadija, and excited about the idea of having a theater event as the man was deeply interested in being part of the workshop. They invited us into their one-room lodging where they served us coffee and shared their story. They had traveled through Turkey and tried to pass unnoticed through Bulgaria, where, when caught by Bulgarian police, they were beaten and their passports were stamped. The stamp marked Bulgaria as the "first safe EU country" to which they arrived – according to the regulations.

That meant it was the only country to which they could legally seek asylum. Hence, in Germany, when they applied for refugee status, they expected to be declined. Nonetheless, with the help of a lawyer they filed for German asylum and were waiting for the ruling at the time of our workshop.

This couple and many other refugees are often very ready to recount their troubles to any willing listener. Their stories have been retold or rehearsed in formal interviews and in informal conversation, with both familiar people and total strangers. The question in applied theater practice is: what can workshops do with those stories and for the refugees?

One of the men (I will call him "Yaser") interested in participating asked me why I wanted to lead this workshop. I explained my vision of the refugees as having undergone a difficult journey and now being suspended in indefinite waiting, and then explained my plan for the workshop to serve as a way to enable participants to tell their stories collectively. Yaser then helped with distributing the flyers at several buildings and on the road. As we greeted residents passing by, we briefly explained the event. Most of the people who seemed to be interested in the workshops were Syrian refugees.

I was not surprised to find willingness among Syrian refugees. Syrians, generally speaking, are predisposed to value theater as a medium. Drama has long been a well-regarded art form in the country: Syria has one of the strongest theater-training academies in the region; Damascus hosted a prestigious international theater festival; and one of the key late twentieth-century Syrian dramatists, Saladah Wannous, was influential across the Arab world. Syrians do not need much convincing that participating in a theatrical endeavor is worthwhile.

After the recruitment tour, we had approximately 15 committed participants who had shown interest, and the workshop was only two days away. That group consisted of men only, which was not planned as the invitation was clearly addressed to include both men and women. After discussing this with one of the center administrators, I learned that most of the newly arrived refugees came with patriarchal thinking: one recent study conducted by Krabbe found that Syrian refugees' masculinity could be either overcompensated or adapted (2017, p. 8).

It seems that the group I met at the refugee center was more on the overcompensated side. The fact that they were in Germany did not mean for them that they would forget their conservative behavioral patterns, which included excluding women from participating in workshops or outings alone. I perceive this as an ongoing challenge for anyone doing this type of work with refugees from conservative cultures. While acknowledging that this as a challenge, applied theater practitioners should actually always be ready to adapt their plans and accommodate the communities that they are serving and find ways to lead dialogue with them even if the community exhibits a behavior that others may disagree with. Within this spirit, I do not find it harmful to lead a workshop for all-male participants knowing that their partners or wives are at the center waiting for them.

Eager to get this workshop under way, I started preparing myself, and I also began prepping Khadija, as it would be her first applied theater workshop. I explained to her the games I would be using and how to handle her presence while in the workshop. For example, if she was not part of the activities, she would need to take notes on the exercises, and in case she was part of the activities, she would need to yield her voice to the participants. I was very detailed when I explained to her the contested question in applied theater concerning process versus product. In particular, workshop facilitators and leaders are always asking: *Should the workshop culminate in a formalized stage presentation for an audience, or is this art for its therapeutic value?*

As an applied theater practitioner, I am always cautious about having a final performance for the workshops I lead. I try my best not to have a final performance for a large audience; however, I usually agree to have a small presentation, pending the approval of the participants. Even then, audience members are selected carefully. Having an intimate presentation for a supportive audience can contribute to empowering the participants and validating their discussions in the workshop because they will have a platform where they may publicly share fragments of their work. Writing about applied theater in prisons, Lisa Biggs explains that a workshop combined with a performance might enhance the benefit to the participants, allowing them the chance to be heard by a public audience, and it can also constitute "counter rhetoric" to the predominant public discourse (Biggs, 2016). Even though the refugees are not in prisons, the analogy is there as both refugees and prisoners are existent within a state of waiting. Prisoners are waiting to leave prison, and refugees are waiting to get residency and to move freely and have their own place.

Whether I advocate for a final performance or not depends mostly on the community I work with, and about the context of the workshop in general. For instance, I recall one of the participants in this workshop expressing that he would not be comfortable acting for a large audience. That comment ended any aspiration, direct or indirect, I may have had for holding a large-scale performance.

Second act: the workshop

The workshop took place in a large room that had movable chairs, flip charts, and markers. Nine participants showed up, all of them males between the ages of 20 and 40. They seemed to know one another as all of them were center residents. Five of the participants were Syrians, one was Palestinian, one was Iraqi, and two were from Eritrea. All participants except for the two from Eritrea spoke Arabic fluently; therefore, as I started the workshop, I began to provide instructions in a mix of Arabic and English to ensure that the two Eritrean participants were fully engaged.

While participants were gathering, some were very curious to know about me. Questions ranged from my age to what I was doing in Germany to why I was not applying for refugee status. I explained that I am from a small town in Syria, close to Damascus, and that I had lived during the past 12 years in the U.S. and Jordan. The participants' questions touched on another factor that applied theater practitioners need to consider: what side of myself do I show to workshop members? How much personal information should I share? By sharing my personal information, I was seeking to gain their trust. Because I too had left my homeland to live elsewhere (although under less difficult circumstances), I thought my background might provide some common ground between the men and me. At the same time, I knew that there was the risk that the men might be cautious about my intentions, as many of the participants were still afraid that I might have been planted by some political entity to get to know about them and report them to the Syrian or German government. It was important for me to assure them that my role as the workshop leader was based on community and social ethics, and not related to governmental politics.

I also introduced Khadija and explained her presence as my assistant. Being attentive to the gender dynamic and having Khadija as the only woman in the room, I talked about her knowledge about Arab culture, thereby adding another level of trust for the participants.

At that point, I had arrived at another question that affects workshops, but this one must be posed directly to the participants: whether or not we may document the event by photography or video. Archiving my workshops is usually done for my own sake. I do so to keep track of my work, remembering it, reflecting on it, and learning from it. I asked the group's permission to take photographs, a request that was denied by a couple of participants. When participants deny the request to record them, we do not ask why or try to persuade them otherwise, though we might privately try to guess their reasons. Refusing to be photographed can simply be interpreted as being fearful that the recordings would be seen by Syrian authorities. Many of the participants might still have family in Syria, and if the state knows that they have relatives who have fled, it could jeopardize their safety. I return later to this refusal, in light of participants' overall willingness to expose their experiences across the workshop.

The main body of a workshop involves risk-taking activities, which require a gradual wading in to acclimate participants to using voices and bodies in unusual ways. This raises two fundamental questions all applied theater practitioners face when they design workshops. First, *how does the facilitator set ground rules to create a safe place for the kind of unusual behavior participants will engage in, in exercises?* In longer workshops, like some that run over several days, facilitators may spend an hour eliciting rules from the group collectively, but in a six-hour session, this needs to happen more efficiently. In this particular episode, we began the workshop by explaining that some of the games and activities might be funny and require silly behavior. I took a little time to stress the fact that even though they might be laughing and having fun, they should not ridicule anyone during – or after – the workshop. Second, *which exercises should I use as a warm-up for this specific group?* There is a large menu of options, some of which I have studied in practitioner publications, while others I developed by trial and error as I led workshops in different contexts.

I opted to begin with an activity centered on names. With the group standing in a circle, I said my name and then invited everyone to echo my name in unison. After a little bit of hesitation, the singularity of the name in one voice was echoed collectively. At the larger level, I see this small exercise as a representation of the point of the workshop: a public narrative created through individual stories. We modulated the quality of the expression of the name, saying it in slow, angry, happy, or enthusiastic ways.

The vocal warm-up offers the easiest entry to theatrical work, after which it is crucial that participants begin to use their bodies and interact physically, which contributes to the non-verbal aspects of the theatrical expression. I guided the participants into creating a knot with their bodies: they joined hands in a tangle across the circle, and then they had to un-knot the tangle together by turning or crossing individually, interacting with others to figure out the best next move. The fact that only men were participating in the room made it possible for them to venture further into physical activities. This exercise would have been impossible had there been any female participant in the group as it is not acceptable within conventional Arab culture to touch bodies between men and women.

After they untangled the knot, I asked them to move around the room and then come back and form a circle or a triangle, each man standing as a point in the shape, trying to create the shape without verbal interaction. These small, achievable challenges usually generate the participants' individual and collective satisfaction. Metaphorically, the simple exercises suggest something more profound: *We can solve problems, together: we can communicate even without speech, across differences.* To me, that characterizes how applied theater operates more generally. That effect can happen surprisingly quickly. The warm-ups bolster the self-confidence and group trust required for the later storytelling segment.

After the basic warm-up, the workshop does not yet plunge into the core phase but instead shifts to an intermediary phase during which participants face more complex group challenges that involve physical movement or speech in varied ways. Again, I draw exercises from a diverse menu of options. Influenced by Boal's Image Theater (2013), I ask participants to create, and also interpret, "frozen images," in which they hold a pose representing some kind of social dynamic, sometimes literally and sometimes abstractly or symbolically. I asked two men to shake hands and freeze and asked the rest of the group to imagine them as a statue in a museum. I then posed questions to prompt their interpretation: "Are they friends or foes?" and "Their facial expressions are friendly and their body gestures are peaceful, so what is the story behind this frozen image?"

At this phase, I continued altering the image and prompting for spectators' interpretations. I instructed one actor to exit the pose, and then asked the group, "Only one person is frozen – what is the story behind this image?" Some men said, "It is still peaceful." I asked someone else to join the frozen image and create a different energy in the way he decided to shake hands. I asked each of them to state one word or sentence to voice the figure's internal monologue. The speakers conveyed the hostility of the scene, saying, "I will hit you," "Move away from me," or "Enough." After spending that first moment focused narrowly on the dynamic between the two sculpture characters, I guided the group to consider the full scene. I asked the group to speculate about the setting of the frozen image. One responded, "They might be in prison." When I again asked them to voice the unspoken dialogue, some said, "Admit it," or "I have nothing to say." Again, I asked the whole group to voice the internal monologue they could imagine. Some responded, "Do not hit me," and "I will humiliate him."

Sharing stories

After becoming flexible with movement and voice, and having begun to create and interpret images of social scenes, the participants were ready for the next step: collaborating to convey emotion through a simple story. Dividing the large group into teams of three, I asked each team to compose and share a story related to fear and courage. The question of fear and courage was prompted by a workshop I had led in Jordan with Syrian refugees who reside in Jordan. The theme of the workshop was proposed by Rana Kazkaz and Anas Khalaf, who at the time were producing a documentary about Syrian refugees. I found that prompting this question was helpful in encouraging the refugees to share their stories.

The story could be based on an actual event, and I ask them to make it a story of one specific person. I suggested that it could represent their journeys to the camp or their living situations in Germany. I then explained the steps. First, each member would share his single story (whether real or imaginary) in his respective group. Next, each group would either select one story to be shared (by voting) or they could blend their stories into one composite narrative. I gave them 30 minutes to work within their groups. While they were engaged in sharing their personal stories, I circulated among them. At the time the groups were getting ready to share their stories, I divided the room into two spaces: a performance space and a spectating space. When they were ready, each group took its turn presenting its chosen story in that designated stage space. After their narration, I asked questions, as did other spectators.

The first group shared its story about a group of men leaving Syria. The men had decided to make the trip to Germany taking a route through Macedonian forests, but while they were in the forest walking, one of the men became injured. Thinking he would die, he implored his friends to send messages to his mother asking her for forgiveness. He told his travel companions that if he died on the road, he wanted his body to be taken back home to Syria, and for one second the group discussed which route they would take if that happened – they were willing to stop their trip and return on his behalf.

I asked the performing group whether they felt courage or fear, and they answered that they felt fearful when the man asked his companions to send greetings to his mother, and they felt courageous when the men decided to carry him through the forest. A spectator asked the actors if their characters at any point felt that they already had their own problems and maybe considered leaving the injured man. The actors' answer was, "When you go on such a trip, you meet strange people but you develop a sense of community right from the beginning of the trip and when you walk/eat/sleep – you do that all as one single group, so the idea of leaving him behind was never present."

I asked the team which incident from this story they would decide to dramatize during the rest of the workshop. The answer was the moment of choice: when the other refugees decided to help the injured man – a group of men who were abandoning their lives back home and moving forward, going to all the trouble to reach Germany, and getting so close, yet who were willing to return to Syria to fulfill the injured man's death wish. That moral decision was for them a dramatic moment.

The second group decided to share two stories that involved a different set of refugees whose story followed a different geographic path. In this case, a group left Eritrea and traveled to Sudan, and from Sudan to Libya where they were transported in a small, cramped truck, so crowded that they felt they would fall off at any moment. During most of the trip, they were hungry and thirsty. According to them, Arabs in Libya make problems for Eritreans who do not speak Arabic. They were among 600 refugees in Libya staying in a small house for 20 days, waiting for their turn (for the trafficker to call them) to go on to Italy. When their turn came, they found themselves on a ship with a capacity of 150 people but that was carrying 700. After this group told their stories, I asked them to identify which parts were associated with fear or courage. Most of them said they felt the most fear in Libya, although one said he felt courageous then.

In the same workshop, there was one Iraqi man who shared a second story, and it was his own story about how he used fake passports to travel across four countries, from Turkey, to Tanzania, Brazil, and Spain, until he arrived in Germany. He later explained that fear arose every time he was at an airport because he was traveling with fake passports. He felt courageous only when he arrived in Spain. Upon reaching Madrid, his fellow travelers (he was traveling in a group) left him. He was disappointed that his companions – friends and relatives – were leaving him, but back home they had told him that once they reached Europe, each one would be responsible for his own fate. He felt courageous, telling them they could leave him. "I will figure it out myself," he had said. He had not known what to do, so he called friends in Germany who sent him money to hire a car to bring him to them.

The third group told two stories that centered on migrations from Syria. In one, a father and his four children, including a 1-year-old daughter, walked from Turkey to Bulgaria, crossing a thorny forest. He did not know if he was walking in the right direction. He reached a checkpoint where the Bulgarian police caught them and asked from where they had come. When they said they were from Syria, the police inspected them and then called the Red Cross. They put them in a camp with very poor living conditions and gave them a three-year residency in Bulgaria. But the father wanted to move on and took his children in a truck to Hungary and then to Germany.

Another story was about a man serving in the Syrian army, who ran away to Iraq and then to Turkey. He tried to connect with a smuggler for about a month, with no results. He decided to bring his wife, who had to be smuggled into Turkey across the Syrian border. The hardest thing for him was when he knew she was nearby – only across the border – but she had lost connection with him. That kept him very worried about her for one day until she arrived. After that, they were smuggled to Bulgaria, where they were caught by Bulgarian police, who beat them.

The transition from the preliminary stories to a performance raises other questions of technique: should participants *act* or speak dialogue, or should they convey events and emotions through images? To answer these questions on the spot, I resort to what Michael Balfour (2016) calls the "social instinct" of the facilitator which can be defined as the ability of the facilitator to pick up the best in a group and determine where the workshop is heading based on immediate observation to the participants' dynamic, and the ability to respond on the spot with sensitivity and respect. Following my social instinct in preparing for the workshop presentation, I decided not to ask participants to act out the stories dramatically. The intensity of the stories and the emotions that were racing to the surface made me aware that the group was not interested in acting them out. They already knew their stories, and I believed that acting out the whole story would just make them worried about getting it right "theatrically," while it was clear that they needed to express their feelings in a different way.

I asked them, therefore, to compose three group frozen images based on Boal's and Rhod's frozen-images techniques that symbolized their stories. Each image would last for five seconds, and then they would shift into the next image. Each performer in the image would state a sentence that would describe their action and express their emotions. Some sentences were said in a repetitive way, and other sentences were just stated once neutrally. For example, for an image that looked like a man carrying a child while someone is attacking him while someone is watching, the men described the actions: one said, "I am carrying the child"; another said, "I am police; I would not let him cross the border"; and the third said, "I am a bystander and can't believe what is happening and I feel powerless."

To articulate a scene in which the men are carrying what seems to be a wounded man, the performers said, "I am helping my friend . . . I am going up to the truck to keep going on the road . . . I am asking him to hurry up . . . I am the smuggler and collecting the money." Other statements expressed suffering – "I am hungry"; "We are tired"; "I am so sick" – or the interests of the traffickers: "I want money."

To frame the final presentation, I asked them to present their images together at the beginning; then each group displayed its images alone. At the end, they combined the images together as a final product. It all took about five minutes, and we had one audience member who happened to come by, Professor Gordon Mitchell, from the University of Hamburg. His presence added a performative flavor to the presentation since the workshop participants were "acting" for an outsider.

After the presentation ended, we all sat in a circle for a final reflection during which I asked each of them to say anything related to the experience they had had together that day. The conversation centered on their present as they noted, after all the humiliation that they had faced in Hungary and Bulgaria, when these refugees reached Germany, they felt that they had reached their target. However, the minute they arrived they started facing other challenges. One of the challenges was that they felt the laws are not applied evenly. For example, two men had undergone the same trip, submitted the same kind of asylum application, and waited for about nine months. Yet one of them was given residency, while the other was rejected. When the one who was rejected filed an appeal, he found himself "back to zero." He needed to start the process all over. According to these narrators, Germany has a good reputation in executing the law, but two judges might have different opinions for the same rule. One explained, "When you reach Germany, you indeed forget all the difficulty of the trip but you start another journey of waiting and psychological suffering. Every minute you wait here equals all the suffering of the trip." I asked them, "What makes you keep going?" The answers were: "You want to settle. You want to *live*. You want to have a future for your children."

Was it worth it?

Even though most of the participants expressed positive attitudes toward the workshop, the effect of telling and stylizing stories is not always felt as positively and may run some risks for participants. After the rounds of images and interpretations, I asked the group, "You tell the same stories all the time. How is it different for you to tell it now?" Two men's answers encapsulate the strengths and risks of this kind of narration technique. One said, "I feel it is comforting. It is not only telling the story by talk." However, another said, "I feel bad, because I remember all what I have gone through."

The comment of that participant still haunts me as an applied theater practitioner. How can I balance bringing up a painful memory while framing that memory as a learning experience without bringing the participant down as it did in my workshop? But doesn't reliving the experience, however painful, constitute the first step in overcoming it? How would the same participant feel about this experience the next day?

While leading this workshop and other workshops based on storytelling, I keep asking myself as well about the way in which telling life stories in a theater workshop format is different from telling stories in participants' everyday lives. These stories have been told many times, on different occasions. They have been told in private settings, such as when meeting friends in the reception center, as well as during interviews with officials through the residency application process. In a study by Alison Jeffers (2008), she argues that personal narratives presented in what she calls "bureaucratic performances," meaning while being interviewed by refugees case officers, are told in a way that focuses on presenting the refugee as a victim. Conversely, presenting these stories within an applied theater workshop would focus on countering the victimhood notion and turning it into championing their refugee experiences. In addition, when stories are told in a theater workshop format, while they are told in a space that is not exactly public, participants are nonetheless sharing the stories in a civic space among peers outside the family. Unlike asylum interviews or border interrogations, the workshop allows them to control the form and style of their narration. Sharing their stories with peers allows them to be more aware of details of their experiences. This story exchange also allows them to recognize shared patterns among different stories, a way of recognizing their common experiences despite their differences.

The participants were open. and one might say generous, in sharing their stories. I want to juxtapose that generosity with their desire not to be seen, as when some men refused to be photographed at the beginning of the workshop. I think we can read their understanding of the workshop narration as safe, relative to the lasting effect of visual images. The participants became aware during the workshop that they were building a composite narrative out of the individual stories they had told and re-told, which they would perform once in the moment. As a *collective* narrative, it would avoid the singularity of one person's story, whereas a photograph would capture a recognizable individual. As *ephemeral*, the performances would not last and travel, while photographs could reach authorities back home.

Finally, taking charge of their stories and sharing them in a creative way empowers them and gives them agency. Their stories are told in this workshop with a specific intention, an intention that is grounded in the aesthetic of a theatrical performance. As Bundy (2003) claims, in an aesthetic experience that involves both cognition and emotions, this interaction will result in a new understanding of their place in the world for the participants. The new understanding the participants take away from the workshop will hopefully have a positive impact on their connection with their new lives and empower them to look forward, past the traumas they have experienced. Taking charge of their stories within an applied theater format will hopefully give them the sense of agency they need while they are transiting their lives.

References

Balfour, M. (2016). The Art of Facilitation: 'Tain't what you do (it's the way that you do it).' In S. Preston (Ed.), *Applied Theatre: Facilitation* (pp. 151–164). London: Bloomsbury.

Biggs, L. (2016). Serious Fun at Sun City: Theatre for Incarcerated Women in the "New" South Africa. *Theatre Survey, 57*(1), 4–36.

Boal, A. (1995). *The rainbow of desire: The Boal method of theater and therapy.* London and New York: Routledge.

Boal, A. (2013). *Theater of the oppressed* (C. A. McBride, Trans.). New York: Theater Communications Group.

Bundy, P. (2003). Aesthetic engagement in the drama process. *Research in Drama Education: The Journal of Applied Theater and Performance, 8*(2), 171–181. doi:10.1080/1356978030833

Clayton, J., & Holland, H. (2015, December 30). *Over one million sea arrivals reach Europe in 2015* (T. Gaynor, Ed.). UNHCR. Retrieved from www.unhcr. org/5683d0b56.html

Gallagher, K. (2015). Responsible art and unequal societies: Towards a theory of drama and the justice agenda. In *Drama and Social Justice* (pp. 67–80). Routledge.

Hinger, S. (2016). Asylum in Germany: The making of the 'crisis' and the role of civil society. *Human Geography*, *9*(2), 78–88. doi:10.1177/194277861600900208

Jeffers, A. (2008). Dirty truth: Personal narrative, victimhood and participatory theater work with people seeking asylum. *Research in Drama Education: The Journal of Applied Theater and Performance*, *13*(2), 217–221. doi:10.1080/13569780802054919

Krabbe, B. M. J. (2017). *Masculinities in conflict: A research about the affected masculine identities of Syrian refugees* (Master's thesis). Utrecht University, Utrecht, Netherlands.

Rohd, M. (1998). *Theater for community, conflict & dialogue: The hope is vital training manual*. Heinemann Drama.

Rousseau, C., Gauthier, M.-F., Lacroix, L., Alain, N., Benoit, M., Moran, A., . . . Bourassa, D. (2005). Playing with identities and transforming shared realities: Drama therapy workshops for adolescent immigrants and refugees. *The Arts in Psychotherapy*, *32*(1), 13–27. doi:10.1016/j.aip.2004.12.002

Rousseau, C., Singh, A., Lacroix, L., & Measham, T. (2004). Creative expression workshops for immigrant and refugee children. *Journal of the American Academy of Child & Adolescent Psychiatry*, *43*(2), 235–238.

Spindler, W. (2015, December 8). *2015: The year of Europe's refugee crisis*. UNHCR. Retrieved from www.unhcr.org/en-us/news/stories/2015/12/56ec1ebde/2015-year-europes-refugee-crisis.html

4   The United States

Serving the refugee, connecting with the community

In this chapter, I talk specifically about my work with refugees in Philadelphia. During this period, I was very keenly focused on the therapeutic use of applied theater and its application within the field of drama therapy. The shift in the nature of my work was not intentional; rather, it was a natural progression in response to the needs of the targeted communities with which I was working within a specific geographic location, in this case, the U.S. Before elaborating on the specifics of my work in Philadelphia, I outline some of the main differences between refugees in Germany/Europe and those in the U.S. After firsthand interaction with organizations that work with refugees in both Europe and the U.S., and based on my ethnographic observations, I can outline the following differences. Please note that I am purposely excluding comparison to refugee work in Jordan and the Middle East in general, as there are obvious considerations of linguistic and cultural natures that render these cases, in fact, incomparable.

*   In Europe, asylum-seeking and immigration processes are managed primarily through governmental organizations. The German model depends on distributing refugees to different towns and cities, and each municipality is then responsible for their resettlement. While there are some non-governmental organizations (NGOs) and churches that help, the majority of the work is orchestrated by both national and local government authorities.
*   The role of the American authorities in processing refugee applications is extensive and time consuming at the outset, but governmental involvement swiftly begins to diminish the minute the refugee arrives in the U.S. Among the Syrian refugees I worked with in Philadelphia, for example, the American government worked for about two years on selecting and vetting their applications; then they would hand them over to non-profit organizations, such as what was formerly known as

the Hebrew Immigrant Aid Society (HIAS), which would take over and begin preparing the refugees to find jobs.

• While the question of linguistic and social integration and assimilation is essential in Europe, the question in the U.S. is instead on how to help refugees find employment and provide them with the tools to economically engage with their communities. In Germany, the focus of the government's program is on integrating through German-language courses. While learning the dominant language is crucial to successful integration, it is a complex process with many limitations. Ideally, and in both contexts, this stage should include working with refugees on their post-traumatic stresses.

• The question of language is seemingly absent from the integration process of the U.S. This is, instead, a task that non-profits take on themselves. After refugees have some basic facility with language, they are often referred to an outside language program. In the case of HIAS in Philadelphia, this may be the local community college.

• Another difference in the ways in which the U.S. and Europe deal with refugees is simply related to the logistics of organizing and accepting the volunteers who work with refugees. When I was working with refugees in Germany, I was at the time a visiting researcher at Free University of Berlin. This was a prestigious position that allowed me to visit refugee centers and introduce myself. After a couple of meetings, I would be granted access to the refugee center and the refugees, and granted permission to organize and lead my workshops there.

• The U.S., on the other hand, or at least in my experience, has a far more bureaucratic process in place. To work with refugees, I had to provide a series of local and federal security clearances and attend volunteer workshops – a process that took about three months – before I was listed as a volunteer and given access to lead workshops.

Having all the aforementioned information in mind, I decided to start my work with HIAS by asking some initial questions; these questions would help me later to outline the nature and the scope of my work.

Initial questions

After presenting the clearances and attending the volunteer training workshops, I began sending emails, making phone calls, and pitching proposals to the staff at HIAS to lead workshops with the refugee communities that they were serving in Philadelphia. I finally received an email asking me to lead a workshop with a group of refugees who live in Philadelphia. I asked the normal questions while preparing for my workshop with them: *How many refugees would be there? What is the age range? Their English level? Where are they from? And for how long is the workshop?* These questions are essential for my work in applied theater, especially when working with refugees, for the following reasons:

1   The number of participants would determine the games and exercises I would be leading with them in terms of form and content. Some games are designed for a small number of participants, and other games are designed for a large number of participants. There are games that can create a general positive energy without getting into the details of each and every individual's life, and there are games that focus entirely on the individuals.

2   The age range would determine my approach and level of "playfulness." Most refugees, from a purely international perspective, come from Global South regions where it may be relatively unacceptable for adults to engage in over-the-top physical exercises. Being "playful" in the workshop would undermine the dignity of the participants.

3   The level of fluency in English would determine how verbally heavy my intervention would be. Can I utilize games that depend on extensive oral communication, or should I employ games that allude to the verbal but not depend on it? Asking where the group is from would also determine the linguistic and cultural approach for my workshop. Having a group of refugees from Arabic-speaking countries would allow me to lead the workshop in the Arabic language. In this context, it would, again, be "verbal" heavy.

4   The length of the workshop is very important as it would determine how much time I would allocate to each stage of the workshop organization. How long would the warm-up be? How would I organize the time?

These questions typically lead me to better understand my target audience, which is one of the most important things to pay attention to while working in applied theater. When I approach refugees and refugee center administrators in Europe, I have in mind a target audience for the workshop, and that normally consists of the refugees that are housed in the refugee centers or the social workers or language teachers who serve the refugees. Because refugee centers do not exist in the U.S. as they do in Europe, accessing refugees in a centralized, domestic location was not possible.

When I approached HIAS in Philadelphia, I proposed to work with either the refugees or the English teachers who work with refugees, as I proposed to lead a program to train teachers on how to use drama as a tool to teach English. I was pleased to receive a response from HIAS that they would actually be interested in me leading work with both, and I wound up leading one workshop for their English teachers in addition to leading workshops with multiple refugee groups. The positive response from HIAS reflects an eagerness to form a pro-refugee front that resists the current political discourse that reinforces negative messages about the presence of refugees in the U.S.

Refugees, refugees, refugees

The questions of whether to accept refugees, at what number, and from what parts of the world were some of the key talking points in politics and in the public sphere in the U.S. from 2017 when I most recently returned there and began working with HIAS. The 2016 election of Donald Trump and his espousal of radical views on this issue fueled the flames of discourse. The same questions were simultaneously the absolute center of the public discourse in Germany as well as the rest of Europe, especially after the influx of refugees who fled to Europe circa 2015.

The commitment of the Merkel administration in Germany to host more refugees created significant controversy between political parties. On the other hand, the U.S. in its nature is multicultural, with no official language mentioned in the Constitution and a relatively new sense of American cultural identity. As I have mentioned, the main issue of concern in European politics is the question of "integration," a lifelong argument that the current policies of most European countries agreed to answer by teaching language to the refugees. The question of language-first integration is not present in the U.S., at least within the refugee communities I have interacted with. What is important within the U.S. is finding a job. While learning the language is a prerequisite for getting a job in Europe, many jobs in the U.S. can be found without the need to learn English. The market in the U.S. values an individual's skills and his or her willingness to contribute to the economic welfare of the nation – while simultaneously avoiding taking economic advantage of U.S. citizens – more than whether the person is a refugee or not.

In such a climate, the discourse surrounding refugees is heavily represented in the media, on talk shows, and at academic conferences. But on the ground, it carries less visibility (it took me lots of research on the ground in Philadelphia to learn about the work of HIAS). This could explain why there are fewer plays, movies, and public performances about refugees in the U.S. than in the EU. In Europe, theater has become an outlet, as Philippe Wehle (2005) describes, to "shed lights" and make the stories of refugees "heard." There is simply not the same urge in the U.S. for this to happen.

Applied theater or traditional theater

Before I sent my volunteer proposal to HIAS, I was actually considering a different proposal, to start a theater company that would be geared toward publicly presenting traditional performances to audiences in the Philadelphia area. I was inspired by a study by Liwhu Betiang (2010), documented in the article entitled "Theater of Rural Empowerment: The Example of Living Earth Nigeria Foundation's Community Theater Initiative In Cross River State, Nigeria." In this piece, Betiang describes how the Living Earth Nigeria Foundation (LENF) Community Theater initiated a participatory program for rural towns in Nigeria. The foundation aimed to establish community-based drama troupes; to train the groups in theater preparation, production, and performance; to train them on how to tell their own stories; and to equip them with performance techniques as well as management skills. The method of training included bringing in members with previous artistic talents and experiences, with a focus on using local resources and stories that connect with the local culture. In the end, positive results were seen, where "the quality of cultural life" improved and a general sense of local empowerment, confidence, and awareness, particularly about environmental issues, was achieved.

After conducting so much work in applied theater in Jordan and Germany, where the aim of each workshop was to stay closed and not to have a public presentation, the idea of establishing a community-based drama troupe enticed me. I was hoping that working with HIAS would bring another level of public sharing where I could engage the general public of Philadelphia, where I live for now, in these discussions. I also felt that because I live in a city that is politicized, combined with the relative freedom of speech allowed in the U.S., I could create a theater troupe able to motivate the general public. I recall in this instance Betiang, who states that

> there are indicators that some of the [Nigerian] communities have truly adopted drama as a tool for community development; they are picking up topics relevant to themselves on various fields of life – not only on forestry. Theater is not only an awareness raiser but a tool for mobilization.
>
> (Betiang, 2010, p. 66)

My proposed theater troupe was designed not only to have an effect on the public of the host community but also on the refugees themselves. Even though the work can positively benefit each participant's well-being, it is expected that the work can also have a social impact if members of the host community identify with messages carried through the refugee narratives.

The work can mobilize the community and build awareness by putting the refugees' stories in the public arena, motivating the host community to actively participate, not only as spectators but also in dialoguing about the challenges that refugees face.

In an article entitled "The Politics of Participation: Un Voyage Pas Comme Les Autres Sur Les Chemins De L'Exil," Susan C. Haedicke (2002) describes a performance about the refugee experience that she attended in 1999 in Paris. She explains that the spectating bodies were transformed into performing bodies, and audience members went through a process of identification with the refugee experience through participation. In this experience, the spectator is no longer a neutral bystander but a witness to the experience. Even though the experience did not encourage Haedicke to "do" something, her perspective on immigration policies were "transformed" and she was able to view them through different lenses. Haedicke's article heightens my awareness of the possibilities of aesthetic theater and its efficacy in "transforming" the spectators and members of the host community.

My desire to create a theater company to present refugee stories was further rooted in the fact that I believe that a dialogue about refugee issues on the grassroots level is imperative. I believe that the general public must connect the specific, personal stories of refugees to the detached political discourses that happen around refugees. In all of my work, I want to create a different knowledge that speaks to what Helen Cahil (2014) calls "theater for enquiry." In her article "Withholding the Personal Story: Using Theory to Orient Practice in Applied Theater About HIV and Human Rights," Cahill explains what she calls "theater for enquiry" as a process that resists having a final answer and instead encourages a culture of questioning. According to Cahil, theater for enquiry depends on three pillars: critical enquiry, creative enquiry, and collective enquiry. She further explains that under such conditions, where change could be a possibility, the theater setting becomes a place where knowledge is both created and exchanged.

Despite my heightened appetite for starting a theater company for refugees, with the aim of taking the audience on a journey through displacement, my primary goal remained continuing my work with refugees in whatever capacity possible. Through this connection and the work that ensued thereafter, I made an important discovery: the challenges I faced with refugees from HIAS were no different than the challenges I faced elsewhere, and starting a theater company was unlikely.

First, refugees with whom I worked through HIAS were mostly in their first year of the refugee experience, and they were still navigating an overwhelming amount of paperwork; because this entails a lot of time, it puts the refugees in the same holding pattern of uncertainty that refugees in the centers of Germany or the camp cities of Jordan experience. They are not sure if their paperwork will go through and whether they may have to move after it is approved. For this reason, many are reluctant to engage in meaningful assimilation, as they are uncertain that the city or even the country will be a place of permanent residence.

Second, most of the refugees come from countries where art in general and theater in particular are frowned upon and are considered socially unacceptable. Under this singular condition, it takes a tremendous amount of time to make participants comfortable enough to begin even the tamest of theater games. In a short-term workshop, I am able to make much less progress with participants than when theater is a valued and intrinsic form of human expression within the native culture.

Third, most of the refugees, if not all, were experiencing financial constraints and were far more focused on finding employment and/or wanting to learn the language. For these reasons, as well, they were not in the frame of mind to join an unestablished theater troupe.

My excitement about creating a theater troupe, and my awareness of the challenges to achieving it, went hand in hand with my growing doubts about the efficacy of applied theater work. Given the limitations of being a non-citizen and non-resident alien in the U.S., I realized that the theater company would have to wait. If I were to work with refugees in the immediate future, I would need to follow through on the connection I established with HIAS.

Limitations of applied theater

One of the issues that comes to my mind whenever I practice applied theater with refugees is whether theater can actually create a healing force in the lives of the people who are going through drama therapy. This limitation is shared in the work of Sophie Tamas (2012) in her article "Writing Trauma: Collisions at the Corner of Art and Scholarship," in which she chronicles her own experience of spousal abuse. Tamas consistently acknowledges being lost and stuck, an aspect that most survivors share while attempting to communicate trauma. Tamas also makes a note on the use of art in therapy and trauma, and how it cannot always lead to positive conclusions, that trauma can sometimes be too complex to be "solved" and resolved by art. This limitation that Tamas describes is felt in many moments of my practice, particularly when engaged in small talk with participants both before the workshops and after.

I recall here a conversation I had with Ahmad, a Syrian refugee who resides in Philadelphia.

Ahmad is in his late 50s, and he was so hesitant to participate in a workshop which included physical activity that he seemed to be physically uncomfortable doing it. He met with me for coffee a couple of days after the workshop and explained to me that his reluctance to participate was because he felt that the movements in the workshop, however simple, were not socially appropriate for a man of his age. He then told me that despite this, doing the minimal movements during the workshops made him feel "good" and "positive," a feeling that stayed with him for a couple of days after the workshop. He then went on to tell me details about the way he managed to make it to the U.S.

While listening to Ahmad, a series of images began flickering in my head: images of the tents of Zaatari Camp where he first landed after fleeing Syria, the desert he crossed before finally arriving in Jordan, the sand, running in the night, three days in a small prison at the Jordanian border, and much more about the UNHCR employees who finally selected him for transfer to the U.S. In the middle of Ahmad's story I began to think, perhaps for the first time in many years of working with refugees, *how can I expect a workshop or a series of workshops to create a solid effect for someone who has experienced this much loss and trauma?*

Sophie Tamas presents an excellent metaphor about the kind of work we do in the field. In scene six of her article, Tamas suggests that the traumatized is something like a broken edifice. In the case of the refugee, we could say they are structural ruins from the war. The act of storytelling by a trauma survivor, says Tamas, is like a flower growing in ruins. This metaphor repositions the idea of repairing the ruins to fix them and put broken pieces back in place. She says doing this "tries to find a way to speak of loss without obscuring it" (2012, p. 44). It puts the process of recovering from trauma and using art as a tool for this in perspective of what the storyteller is trying to achieve for himself or herself. Thinking of traumatic storytelling like this allows a space of comfortable healing as opposed to the pressure of finding a resolution.

Another limitation of applied theater work is related to the concept of empowerment and the possible countereffects of the work if we present potentials of change without having the right context for that change to take place. In "Here We Are: Social Theater and Some Open Questions about Its Developments," Guglielmo Schininá (2004) writes about the use of empowerment as a tool of applied theater and advises practitioners not to facilitate creative processes that will lead to empowerment if the conditions of the group will make it hard for them to achieve it. In that case, it will be expected that the work will have a countereffect if the participants are exposed to the potential of better conditions but do not have the actual logistics to achieve them.

Despite these limitations, I believe that working with refugees will also have a positive effect on their lives on many levels.

1   It allows them to articulate their narratives in a creative way.
2   It allows them to bond with one another and form new friends, whether they are living in a refugee center or in a new city.
3   It gives them a break from the concerns of their lives and helps them envision new life options.
4   It helps them make sense of their pasts.
5   It helps them to re-envision their future.

The other kinds of limitations that accompany applied theater work are related to aesthetics. What kinds of aesthetics are we creating? Is an aesthetically pleasing product the means or the goal of the work? Is applied theater "theater" at all if it does not have spectators? Are aesthetics alone able to raise awareness? While it is generally agreed upon that the ultimate goal of applied theater is the well-being of the people involved, aesthetics therefore should be a means to achieve that goal and not a goal in itself.

Aesthetics

While describing the connection between the interventional and aesthetic theater, Anthony Jackson (2005) states that theater that is applied, whether used in social centers or in educational settings, can have both aesthetic and interventional values. He does not indicate that they are both needed, but that unless there is a strong aesthetic value for the work, the interventional implications would be similarly absent. I agree with Jackson, and I even argue that one of the differences between the psycho-social support sessions and the drama therapy sessions is the blossoming of aesthetic moments during the drama therapy sessions. These moments can be perceived as magical and transformative; I call them "poetic moments," as they transfer the applied theater practitioner or drama therapist and the refugee into a new territory that is neither theatrical nor therapeutic.

I recall one of the workshops in Philadelphia where I was working with a couple of refugees from Syria, and the point of the workshop was to get them to identify moments of fear and hope during their escape from Syria to Turkey. One of them, Aya, talked about the days when she was trapped in a smuggler's apartment on the border between Syria and Turkey. She said that the smuggler asked her to stay in a small room and keep her phone on. The room was used as a station for fugitives like her who want to be close to the border, but well hidden. There was a small window high up in the room. She would wait for the breeze to pass by the window and would take a deep breath. That was her moment of hope, that moment of breeze.

After hearing this story, I continued to imagine dramatizing it with Aya. As a theater artist who can see potential in such moments, I was struck by the imagery of the scene she recalled: the narrative, the sound, the movement. If I had been able to form my theater company, I would have worked on this narrative with Hanan by creating a scene that prepares the audience for this moment, telling all the backstory and the given circumstances that led to it. When reaching that denouement, when Aya would feel the breeze and take a long breath, I would ask her to stop talking and play music for her while she is reminiscing on that feeling, reliving it, rebreathing it. Even though that moment of narrative recollection was inspired in a small workshop and did not have any spectators or outside audiences, I am reminded that taking the time to create that aesthetic moment would have had reaching impacts. That is the kind of work we want applied theater to represent. These are the stories that applied theater can utilize to change the public's view of the world.

I claim that arts in general and applied drama in particular have the potential to offer participants a site where their emotions can be presented in an "aesthetic" way. Sharing their personal stories, and through the act of creating an aesthetic correlative, they may objectively view the refugee experience and all of the adherent traumas that accompany it. Further, participants are able to focus on the minute details, crafting them to share them with their fellow workshop participants and a future potential audience. Engaging the personal within an aesthetic frame constitutes an excellent start to talk about the personal from a distance.

The applied theater workshop becomes a space in which the participants will recreate and reflect on their life experiences, an intertwined dual process that happens within the physical space and makes it difficult to open the workshop to outside viewers. Here is where the stark difference between the applied theater workshop setting and the community theater for refugees emerges. Similarly to applied theater, a theater company aimed at supporting a local refugee community will be consistently focused on creating a performance for an audience; a process of reflection will be well embedded in the process of rehearsals, but unlike applied theater, the focus and the weight of the whole experience will be to reach the stage. As a practitioner in the field, I call for other theater practitioners to create both kinds of products, as both of them will be needed for the psychological well-being of the refugees. Applied theater will be the way to dig deeply and process, while aesthetic theater will be an excellent tool to empower refugees by "showing" their talents in a performance format and creating a dialogue in their host communities with locals through the presentation of their narratives.

Addressing trauma and narrative at HIAS

In her article "Writing and Righting Trauma: Troubling the Autoethno-graphic Voice," Sophie Tamas (2009) questions the ethics of working with people who have gone through trauma from an academic perspective. She asks questions on the nature of trauma and its telling to others, as well as the artistic process of this communication in a theatrical setting. Beginning with a brief telling of her own playwriting experience, Tamas addresses the idea of ethically representing characters. She continues, sharing her own studies of trauma and the scholarly and academic perspective on commu-nicating personal experiences in a clean and concise manner. In the end, Tamas concludes that to "properly" talk about trauma in the scholarly sense, the victim must have recovered in order for the enactment and story to be as clean as needed.

This question of ethics hits home for me. When I work with refugees, I am always reminded of my own practice and its implications on me and on the lives of the refugees. The refugees come to my workshops for many reasons. They come initially out of curiosity; they want to see who the workshop leader is, they want to see how they can use theater to enhance their well-being, and they sometimes come just to pass time. I recall here a drama therapy workshop I led in Philadelphia in 2017 in which a Russian woman in her 70s was one of the attendees. She spoke very little English, and she always came to the workshop dressed formally, with ironed dresses and high heels. Her classy clothes and looks could not hide the wrinkles of her hands and face. She used to be a physician in Russia and was now living with her daughter, sharing a small studio apartment in North Phila-delphia. I gathered from her talk that she came to my workshops because she had always dreamed of being a performer at the Bolshoi Theatre in Moscow.

Later and during the workshop, I gathered that she would actually come to the workshop because it was an excuse to leave the home and have a life away from her daughter. She said that she always wanted to be an actress. When she was a little girl she danced and acted all the time for her family and her friends in school. She explained to me that being an actress in Rus-sia is a big deal but when she wanted to go to college, she chickened out. She did not think she was talented enough; she did not think she could make a living as an artist, and her family never encouraged her to do arts. Instead, she went to medical school. She worked for 40 years as a physician, and now she has nothing. She lost everything. The notion of losing everything is a recurring theme in my workshops; most of the refugees I have worked with came to be refugees by force, and most left behind work, family, and community back home. I rarely meet a refugee from Syria who has not been educated or had a business or properties back home, yet I am always amazed by how they talk about their past lives with contentment and acceptance.

As a theater facilitator working with these communities, I am not sure if I can interpret this acceptance as a sign that these refugees are recovered from their trauma. I am not trained to gauge that, and most of these refugees are not going to go through nor plan on going through traditional therapeutic programs. But if I am not looking at my work as therapy, then what is it? I believe that the workshop that I just described becomes a shared expression of "care" where the participants are in a constant caring, expressive mood. They care about themselves doing the exercise in the "right way"; they also care about their voices being true to their stories; and finally, they actually care about listening to one another's stories and sympathizing with them. This shared performative expression of care becomes a subtle tool for the refugee to negotiate his or her identity and to dialogue with others without fear of confrontation or rejection. It is an internal dialogue that is expressed in body movements, shapes, and transformations during the workshop time. Further, it is a dialogue that is needed for the participants to make sense of their experiences and to rationalize their present moment. Their bodies, however different – female, male, old, young, covered, uncovered – become their tools to dialogue and understand.

This utopian environment that is created in the theater workshop contrasts with the harsh reality that refugees typically live in their daily lives, especially while confronting a political discourse that is blinded by concepts of nationalism and exclusion. In a study by Illsa Malkki (1992) entitled "National Geographic: The Rooting of Peoples and the Territorialization of National Identity Among Scholars and Refugees," the author discusses the notions of rootlessness, nationalism, homeland, culture, and identity in refugees. Malkki attempts to clarify and pinpoint the place of refugees and their own self-identity construction in a "new theoretical crossroads." Malkki attributes public reaction to refugees to the non-fluid and non-adaptable concept of nationalism and specifically to nationalist attachments to a particular physical space.

Most of the refugees I have met expressed the idea that they are people without a place. They have lost the geographic places of their homelands, and they do not have a place, physically or metaphorically, in their new surroundings. When discussing the idea of home with another Syrian refugee in Philadelphia, Salma, who is 40 years old and who was a prominent journalist in Syria, said that the idea of home was settled and solid when she was in Syria. She knew where her home was, as she used to live in a big house with her elderly parents and two brothers who never got married (children continue living with their parents until they get married). She started working as a journalist and made a name for herself, though she used to write under a different name to avoid trouble with the government. At some point, one of Salma's friends, who had joined the revolution, was detained for a couple of days. During one of his conversations with the detaining officer, the officer mentioned Salma's name, calling her a "slut" because of her writing. The minute her friend was released, he came to her and told her that the authorities had found out about her and her writing and that she needed to hide.

Salma moved to her uncle's house, which was in the same village she lived in. Two hours after she left her parents' home, two security officers came to the house, asked about her, went over her room, looked into the contents of her computer, and told her family that she was not allowed to travel any more. Salma had to run away, so she arranged to be smuggled across the border to Lebanon. While in Lebanon, she learned that she had developed kidney failure. International organizations that help refugees donated money for her treatment while she waited for her turn to come to the U.S. She has since arrived in the U.S. only to discover that she is not welcome. She was surprised; she had done what she was supposed to be doing, raised her voice, ran away for her life, and meanwhile had had serious health issues. What can she do now? She cannot go back. The place she used to call home is not safe for her any more. She does not have a place here in the U.S., where she believes people hate her, saying she feels it in their eyes. Salma does not have a home.

The story of Salma follows the limited discourse promoted by nationalists and host community opponents of refugees, opponents who say that refugees have no place there. Salma's story highlights a converse difficulty as well, in which she cannot progress in her own sense of belonging because she does not have a "place." Here, the idea of nationalism is actually limiting for both the host community members and the refugees.

Movement and applied theater

While part of my collaboration with HIAS, which has been described in the foregoing examples based on-small group workshops, has depended heavily on oral expression, other episodes of the work depended on dialogue through movement and on using movement as a therapeutic tool.

Ki no Tsurayuki (ca. 872–945), a famous poet and founder of the theory of ancient Japanese poetry, regarded human feelings as the source of all poems. The same can be said of applied theater. It is found that everything comes from the body, the body carries the emotions, the body carries the soul, the body communicates, and the body tells. The body in my workshops becomes a place where information is shared and where ideas and reflections are argued and contested. The body becomes the center of action, ideas, and workshop itself. I keep in mind that the bodies of the workshop participants are the very same bodies that went on boats and that crossed the sea. They are the same bodies that survived and championed. In the case of covered women, they are the same bodies that have been covered, and they are the same bodies that are still covered. They are the bodies that are trying to find their place in a city that is not theirs and often within a representation of womanhood that they do not share with the dominant population. They are still the same bodies that will survive and will prevail. Their bodies are what is left from their lives back home; their bodies are the strength and the only witness to all of the trauma that they have gone through.

During the movement workshops that I have led with refugees in Phila-delphia, reflection and recognition among the participants has been achieved through a simultaneous act of performing the moment and reflecting on it, almost simultaneously. Once, I proposed that the refugees share stories from their lives before they had to leave their homes. They all opted to share stories about their struggles while traveling, for some to a Jordanian refugee camp – a first stop before they were able to make it to the U.S. after a long and exhaustive vetting.

There are many reasons for their decisions to focus on the physical jour-ney of the refugee experience:

Psychological: Refugees whom I worked with were still attached to the refugee center. Most of them had arrived in the U.S. less than a year prior, and their wounds were still fresh. Given the structure of refugee resettlement in the United States, there has been no focus on helping them get beyond their traumatic experiences; however, they are still living and processing their trauma. For them, their story, the story of seeking refuge, is their identity, at least for now. To be more precise, the story of seeking refuge is now an important layer of each indi-vidual's identity that they are still struggling with.

Social: Their stories, however different, are the threads which join them despite their differences and help them build a social narrative. Refu-gees might be coming from very different places in terms of culture, language, and social traditions, yet they all have to learn to be patient until their paperwork is processed, a process we now know might take years. Sharing stories of their trips, which tend to follow the same structure, is a bonding tactic that they use indirectly to accept one another. I would even say that this bond in the case of Syrian refugees becomes in some cases a stronger bond than even their "Syrianhood," because Syrians from different religions and ethnicities would sharing these stories as a way to bond instead of relying on their country of origin as a bonding reference. Workshop participants at HIAS clearly agreed that the life-threatening experience that they had to go through is the strongest bonding thread they had as a community.

The connection of body work with these kinds of painful stories must be enacted without concern for visual appeal. While performing the scenes and frozen images which constitute a major pillar in my movement therapy work, the material that is presented might not be aesthetically "beautiful" in itself, but it has some kind of "substance," a substance that is both inherent in the material and communicated to the rest of the participants who are watching it. In most of my workshops with HIAS, wherever there is a frozen image, there is a sense of weighted gravity that captures the air, and again, this moment is not achieved because of the beauty of what is being performed, but rather it is reached because of the reality of the experience that is being shared within a closed community. For example, when someone is reflecting on their boat experience, the scene being performed becomes a bridge for the rest of the group.

Another aspect of movement in applied theater is what I call the "corporal dialectic" that occurs between the bodies in the workshop site, a dialectic between the social presentation of the story and the personal affiliation to the story. While presenting a frozen image of a family who are on a boat, for example, the family will strike a balance between presenting their personal stories and presenting the social narrative of the refugee experience. The deeper they dig into the details of the personal, the more they strike a nerve with other participants.

I have led workshops on many issues ranging from gender equality in Jordan to workshops on human rights in Egypt; never in my life have I faced a room with heightened emotions the way I saw when leading a workshop with and for refugees while they talked about their experiences while moving to their host community. There is a striking sense of "shared narrative" and "shared emotions" that is not even evident on the surface of refugee interactions, but it is a narrative that the refugees are so interested in sharing, listening to, and seeing. There is a deep desire to witness one another's frozen images and at the same time dig deep into their personal experiences and emotions, finding common elements among what they have faced. There is a deep desire *not* to feel they went through this alone. True, their trips are unique and their stories are very personal, but the shared pattern of their stories, however painful, can serve as an excellent tool to create a camaraderie among them. When they are on the boat, they all become one unit, and a small community is formed. When they walk from Greece to Germany, they try to stick to small groups in which they care about one another. The experience they have endured bridges the gaps among gender, age, religion, and ethnicity. They all transform in one minute into human beings who want to arrive somewhere safe. The experience is overwhelming to the degree that it surpasses all of their differences.

I am not trying to make the refugee experience sound beautiful or ethical; I am just trying to make sense of it, so that both the refugees and the host community can find some shared ground on which to move forward. I am fully aware of many horrible incidents, especially of gender and sexual exploitation that happen among the refugees and between refugees and members of the host community and even volunteers. Not addressing these issues in my workshops and later in my writing does not mean it never existed; it just did not come up in my work with the refugee communities. I argue that opening up for these topics requires more time and personal attention from the facilitator's side and cannot be accomplished in the span of a few days or a week.

The frozen-images exercise locates the thoughts, intentions, and experiences of the bodies of the participants. An embodied dialectic is formed between the participant, her own body, and the other bodies that are in the room, between those who are presenting their formed images and those who are spectating them. The images are unfolding in a process that is both internalized in the thoughts and externalized in the body formation. This dialectic informs the participants that their journey is unfinished yet. They preserved their lives, they arrived at a new home, and a new chapter is to be started. It is a process that they need to fathom and articulate; it is a process that might need a new way of articulating and a new tool that will help them to talk about it. Bodies that are usually covered, neglected, and restrained within an Arab context can and should be moved to become the site of such a process. Participants embrace this new way of processing and trust it as a novel tool to express experience.

When a dialectic process is established between the self/body/group and those who are watching, there is another level of dialectic process that includes conveying the information to the facilitator, in this case, me. I was a facilitator who shares the same language and culture, who is familiar to them. Despite this, as I am reminded in almost every workshop, however they try to transfer their feelings during their experiences, it would be hard for me to fathom what they went through. The facilitator, me in this case, would have another dialectic process to go through, a process of taking his or her findings to the managers of the organization they are working with and sharing their voices there, as managers need to know better so that they can serve the refugees better.

I end this chapter with a thought that brings me back to the center of my work at HIAS – the refugees themselves. Did my workshop help them to achieve better "integration"? Were they able to integrate more readily within their host community? What about their well-being? Their self-esteem?

Their self-regard? As I continue planning for the expansion of that work and the potential of my dreamed-for theater company, I will continue playing these questions through my mind. Until we have clearer answers to them, we cannot effectively address the needs of the most vulnerable citizens of our world.

References

Betiang, L. (2010). Theater of rural empowerment: The example of living Earth Nigeria foundations community theater initiative in cross river state, Nigeria. *Research in Drama Education: The Journal of Applied Theater and Performance*, *15*(1), 59–78. doi:10.1080/13569780903481037

Cahill, H. (2014). Withholding the personal story: Using theory to orient practice in applied theater about HIV and human rights. *Research in Drama Education: The Journal of Applied Theater and Performance*, *19*(1), 23–38. doi:10.1080/13569 783.2013.872427

Haedicke, S. C. (2002). The politics of participation: Un Voyage Pas Comme Les Autres Sur Les Cnemins De L'Exil. *Theater Topics*, *12*(2), 99–118. doi:10.1353/ tt.2002.0011

Jackson, A. (2005) The dialogic and the aesthetic: Some reflections on theater as a learning medium. *The Journal of Aesthetic Education*, *39*(4), 104–118. doi:10.1353/jae.2005.0040

Malkki, L. (1992). National geographic: The rooting of peoples and the territorialization of national identity among scholars and refugees. *Cultural Anthropology*, *7*(1), 24–44. doi:10.1525/can.1992.7.1.02a00030

Schininá, G. (2004). Here we are: Social theater and some open questions about its developments. *TDR/The Drama Review*, *48*(3), 17–31. doi:10.1162/105420 4041667659

Tamas, S. (2009). Writing and righting trauma: Troubling the autoethnographic voice. *Forum Qualitative Sozialforschung/Forum: Qualitative Social Research*, *10*(1). doi:10.17169/fqs-10.1.1211

Tamas, S. (2012). Writing trauma: Collisions at the corner of art and scholarship. *Theater Topics*, *22*(1), 39–48. doi:10.1353/tt.2012.0009

Wehle, P. (2005). Théâtre Du Soleil: Dramatic response to the global refugee crisis. *PAJ: A Journal of Performance and Art*, *27*(2), 80–86. doi:10.1162/1520281053850929

Conclusion
Epilogue

Applied theater and refugee empowerment

It is not altogether unusual to find research on applied theater where the general consensus is that this mode of practice can indeed create a sense of empowerment among community members. I recall here some of the work I saw in Berlin where the focus was on establishing a theater company composed of Syrian youth who had been living in a refugee camp near the city. The work I refer to is that of Alexander Schroeder, a German theater artist who created a theater company for devised performances that focus on presenting the stories of Syrian refugees with whom he has been working. Not only does the theater company create a platform for the refugees to share their stories, but it also encourages the formation of a social capital that stays among them beyond the rehearsal times. Many of the young men formed friendships and were able to support one another.

I remember one participant, whom I will call "Ahmad," telling me after his rehearsal with Alexander that being in the play made him feel like people are finally able to listen to him and his stories. Alexander was not only a director for Ahmad and the group, but also a friend – he would visit with them in the camp all the time and teach them German; he also would take them and other young men to coffee shops and theater events in Berlin. Ahmad told me that he began to feel better about staying in the camp after being in the play and among the group of actors; it was certainly better than waiting and doing nothing. Ahmad told me that he could see his path more clearly.

The sense of empowerment that Ahmad describes could be transformed into action on the ground. Other young people in the camp with Ahmad were even more vocal about the challenging living conditions of the camp and their uncertain future as young refugees. This link between empowerment and mobilization is articulated in Liwhu Betiang's article (2010), as he claims:

> There are indicators that some of the communities have truly adopted
> drama as a tool for community development; they are picking up topics

relevant to themselves on various fields of life – not only on forestry. Theater is not only an awareness raiser but a tool for mobilization.

(p. 66)

These conclusions remind us that there is a link between personal empowerment and social/political mobilization. While not every personal empowerment story will end in political/social activism, almost every social/political activist story started with personal empowerment.

In another study, Morsillo and Prilleltensky (2007) used qualitative methods, including self-reported evaluations and ethnographic observations, to conclude that individual empowerment among high school refugees was increased when the participants were exposed to dramatic activities. The results of the study in respect to activities that involved theater and drama community action showed increased levels of self-expression, assertiveness, socio-political awareness, hopefulness, sense of control, and liberation for individuals; increased levels of independence, acceptance and peer support, and cohesion and solidarity for groups; and finally, general appreciation by the community of youth involvement. The authors claim to have found impact on both participants and audiences alike. They further argue that the refugees felt less hopeless about the community they lived in and had a better understanding of their positioning in the host community.

A meeting with Khaled, a Syrian refugee who was in the same theater group with Alexander Schroeder, demonstrated the same effects that Morsillo and Prilleltensky reported. He noted in the meeting that he is a different person after being in the play with Alexander and the group. He is right; many German artists will come to the rehearsals and will teach them some theater techniques, and they become friends with the group. In the same meeting, Khaled noted that engaging in these dramatic activities built bridges between him and the German community. They understand him more, and he understands them more. This notion of understanding that Khaled is talking about is an important step for inclusion that will move Khaled a step close to active citizenship in his host community.

Other work in support of drama therapy for youth integration is "Classroom Drama Therapy Program for Immigrant and Refugee Adolescents: A Pilot Study" (Rousseau et al., 2007) which presents a study from Montreal on prevention programs for helping refugee and immigrant children work through experiences of loss and trauma. The program was based on drama expression activities, which provided young people with different means for communicating trauma, which they may require if they are limited in their use of the dominant language of the host country – and it also offers a safe space for them to express themselves. The researchers found that the drama therapy that these adolescents participated in improved their school performance and contributed to their well-being in general. The study particularly focused on newcomers, those who had been resident in the host country, with the goal of aiding adolescents in the adjustment process of living in the host country. The purpose of this program "was to give young immigrants and refugees a chance to re appropriate and share group stories, in order to support the construction of meaning and identity in their personal stories and establish a bridge between the past and present" (Rousseau et al., 2007, p. 454).

The connection between the past and the present in the refugee group has proved to be key in my work with refugees. Sharing stories from the past was very helpful, for example, in making meaning from the monologue of Ahmad, a young refugee whom I met in Porto. While describing a workshop I led there, he said that the way the workshop asked him about stories from the past made him happy to share whatever everyone wanted to hear. Everyone was curious about his trip to Porto, and no one ever asked about how life was in Syria before the war. Talking about these past stories and acting them out gave him perspective regarding his current situation and gave him hope that things would be good again.

Ahmad's point is very clear: he was able to transform himself, and it helped him alter his state of awareness. The workshop left him feeling supported by his fellow refugees, and it gave his story legitimacy as he found an audience who listened to him, felt compassion for his story, and felt moved by his words. The workshop gave him a team of supporters and a sense of solidarity that could enhance his well-being.

Monologue work with refugees

While doing applied theater work with refugees, I discovered that devising monologues based on the refugee experience can be an instrumental methodology for allowing refugees to process their journey, pain, and hope. I became inspired to include monologues in my applied theater work after coming across a study that described an auto-ethnographic monologue by a woman named Angela who had recently experienced homelessness. Her work was developed in a program called "Actors Play Themselves." The article, written by Dani Snyder-Young (2011), describes an applied theater program whose goal is to engage audiences in the problems and divisions between the homeless and the housed. The article focuses on the process of constructing Angela's monologue. Through this process, she reconstructs her identity, shifting from victim to survivor. Angela's monologue becomes

> an act of redemption, a way of creating a sober identity in a recovery process, a celebration of survival, a method of educating housed

audiences, a performance of fitness to be a mother for social services agencies. This monologue, like all art, is ambiguous and open ended.

(Snyder-Young, 2011, p. 949)

This vision of monologue work as healing informs my work with refugees. Before one of my workshops in Berlin, I led a pre-workshop discussion with a group of refugees. In this smaller group setting, I asked if they would prefer to dramatize a folk tale or share their personal monologues. In that meeting, Fatima, who is a refugee from Syria, shared that she believed the story of her journey from Syria to Germany was complicated enough for 100 monologues. However, she wanted to share portions of it with a German audience so they could connect with her human experience. She believed that understanding what she had undergone would help them empathize better with refugees.

Working with refugees on personal monologues is not easy because it is *personal*. Many people with whom I have worked assume that the simple fact that I am Syrian means that I gain automatic acceptance into refugee communities. This is true to some extent because of shared language and shared cultural references; however, being from the same country or having a shared language or cultural references will not be sufficient for me to understand what it means for someone to leave their home, hold their child, and get onto the rough sea in a tiny boat not designed for that journey. I need to consistently put myself in check while I am working and remind myself of the privileges I have compared with the community with which I work. This awareness helps me remain sensitive and more acute to the complexities of each refugee's story and to his or her unique social, cultural, and economic positioning in the given host community.

Samer and the refugee habitus

A signature theory in the work of French sociologist and theoretician Pierre Bourdieu (1989) is the concept of habitus and its relationship with capitals in its multiple forms: social capital, cultural capital, and economic capital. These capitals form a basis for the expression of habitus which is presented as a behavior or preference, and the ways in which these capitals are interconnected with the power structure that exists in a given community. In the case of refugees, they arrive in a host community with specific sets of capitals that may have high value in their homelands, but there is no market for their exchange in the host community. A middle-class, educated Syrian who possessed high social status in Syria will face the fact that his life in Germany does not carry the same influence as his life in Syria once did.

In Hamburg, I met a refugee named Samer. He used to be a physician in Syria where he had a successful career, financial stability, and peer respect. When I met him, Samer lived in a settlement center, taking basic German-language classes with other refugees. He was not sure how to have his degree evaluated, an essential step in beginning to look for work. Samer was experiencing despair and hopelessness.

In Samer's case, he had gone to the best university in Syria, Damascus University, and studied medicine there. For the average Syrian, this would have been a tremendous feat. To study medicine in Syria, he would have received the highest grades and competed with many other top students, but the unfortunate turn of events in Syria meant that Samer was now a refugee living in a refugee camp. The *cultural capital* that he possessed in Syria allowed him to enhance his *social capital* there; because he graduated from medical school and had a good job in the top hospital in Syria, he was also able to acquire *economic capital*. All of these capitals that Samer acquired over the years led him to develop a habitus that led him to become one of the social and cultural elites in his hometown.

But, again, Samer is now in a refugee camp in Germany where he has been waiting for almost a year to get his paperwork done. During this time, he has faced many obstacles in taking a formal German-language course, so his learning of the German language has depended on the volunteers who come to the camp and deal with him out of what he perceives to be pity. In Samer's case, he would need one or two years of German courses before even becoming eligible to begin the lengthy process of degree evaluation which could drag on for two or more additional years. During this period, Samer will be ineligible for employment and wholly dependent on the German government for all of his economic needs. His worries do not end with this subsistence living in Germany, because though the government has committed to refugee resettlement, there are countless right-wing groups and individuals who are critical of this social outreach. Given the heightened political environment, Samer and his family are under constant fear of attacks on the refugee complex where he, his wife, and two small children share a one-bedroom apartment. Samer is unable to balance his life here and his past life in Syria. His habitus here and there are so different from each other, and he is rightfully challenged in trying to see a light at the end of the tunnel.

Multiple times, multiple places, same refugee

In conducting applied theater work with refugees, we are typically asked to facilitate the integration of participants into their host communities. As someone working closely with the participants, I often ask myself, *is integration the sole or ultimate goal for refugees?* The dilemma of the integration question is the failure of those pushing this agenda to acknowledge that refugees have left behind families, homes, communities, and memories. Even if the refugees are able to integrate – meaning they are able to master the language of the host community and are able to find a job and pay taxes – would those benchmarks signify authentic integration? All of these practices that are designed to facilitate integration do not take into account the lives of the refugees before they fled to Europe. More importantly, active citizenship is not solely defined by integration itself.

I met with Ahmad, who is a refugee in Germany, and he shared with me that

> after being in a camp for about 6 months, I was finally granted an interview with an officer to determine my case. He was very nice. He asked me about my life in Syria and why I wanted to apply for the refugee status, and he told me that he knows there is a war in Syria and he will grant me the status. At the end, he said, you know, in order to succeed here, you need to forget about your life there.

What Ahmad shared with me is crucial to understanding the refugee's dilemma; they are living bifurcated lives, and the practices of government agencies and many service organizations ignore the reality that refugees are "living simultaneously in two countries" (Fridemann, 2002, p. 311).

The refugee maintains multi-layered linkages to their original countries, and these linkages can be social, economic, cultural, emotional, or institutional, among others (Kelly & Lusis, 2006). We cannot understand the refugee experience without looking at it holistically, as a continuum that connects their lives in their homes with their new lives in their host communities. One critique of the process of "integration" in Europe in general, and in Germany in particular, is the so-called integration focus on one single layer – learning a new language – without consideration for the complexity of the refugee's social and emotional life in their new surroundings.

During the workshops I led in Berlin, I actually met with refugees who were very cryptic about the communication they maintain with their family members in Syria. Many were afraid that maintaining these connections would jeopardize their asylum applications. However, maintaining a social connection with family members is not and should not be a crime. Most of all, communication with parents, children, and even friends should not affect an application for asylum, but the stress that any refugee experiences at the time of application, and because of the various regulations that prevent the refugee applicant from either visiting their homeland or sending or receiving money from their host country – even phone calls or letters – feel like illicit contacts. If government agencies truly intend to support the integration and assimilation of refugees into their host communities, they must first acknowledge that the emotional ties that refugees hold to their home countries go far beyond nostalgia.

Home, homeland, and refugees

Diasporas emerge as people flee, are pushed from, or occasionally migrate intentionally from the geographic origin of their cultural and ethnic communities. Diaspora as we know it in the twenty-first century is an adaptation of the original notion of the Jewish diaspora ushered in by the Roman occupation of Palestine in the first century C.E. The term *diaspora* has gained new meanings within our age, and it is characterized by globalism, transnationalism, and cultural hybridity as argued by Alfonso, Kokot, and Tölölyan (2016) in *Diaspora, Identity, and Religion*. I find that in the case of the Syrian refugee there exists a different understanding of the diasporic notion and its connection to the homeland.

The concept of home and homeland is complicated in the Arabic language as well as within Arab communities. Much as the Greek language designates different words to refer to various kinds of love (*agape*, *philia*, and *eros* being the most common), Arabic language designates different words to describe various notions of home. For example, one would use the term *bait* to refer to the edifice of a home, like the English house. Home, as in homeland, is tied into the phrase *min wein ante*, or "where are you from?" Another word that could describe home is *balad*, which roughly translates as country, but *balad* is also loaded with poetic spirit. Then there is another word that could be used to describe home – *wat'n* – which refers to the national/patriotic element of the country. Finally, there is the Arabic *dar*, which is a more colloquial term, similar to *bait*, or the physical structure of the home.

Building on the work of Gurney and Means (1993) and Mallett (2004), Wilfried Poppe (2010) offers three definitions of home in her article entitled "Habitus and the Reasons and Intentions for Residential Mobility and Home-ownership: A Mixed-Method Study Among Former Refugees in Buffalo." Poppe argues that three definitions for *home* exist: The cultural discourse of home, the physical home, and most importantly the personal experience of imagining, creating, and remembering home. We find these concepts echoed in the refugee use, understanding, and application of home as well.

I often asked the refugees I met in Jordan and Germany about what or where they consider to be home. It has been interesting to witness the various meanings interact with one another in the mind of the refugee.

The Syrian refugees I have met are more likely to actively identify themselves as Syrian in both ethnic and cultural terms. I recall here the words of

Zain, a Syrian refugee I met in Jordan, who told me that in Syria, if someone had asked him "How do you identify yourself?", he would have answered, "I am Arab, Arab Syrian (*arabi sori*)," but after he left Syria and after the suffering, pain, and distress of being a refugee, he does not even want to address himself as Arab. He sees himself here as Syrian only.

While leading workshops with youth in Zaatari Camp in particular, their conceptions of home are probably the most striking I have experienced. At Zaatari Camp, thousands and thousands of people are living in the desert in tents. Some are able to leave the camp one way or another, but many reside there for years. It becomes home for them. While refugees in Zaatari Camp are restricted by the physicality of the fenced-off area and the construction of tents and now trailers, you can still sense that a community is evolving there. For example, there are shops, markets, and designated tents for children to play in under the supervision of the countless international organizations that volunteer there. The resignation of Zaatari's refugees to a permanent life in the camp is palpable. Residents have created places that resemble home for them; however, it is not home, not even in the most basic understanding of *dar* or *bait*.

Religion, refugees

Religious scholar Thomas and Tweed (1997) studies the importance of religious symbols, artifacts, shrines, and practices. His work examines how these cultural artifacts create a connection between the homeland and the new land, creating a bond between diasporic individuals and communities. Large numbers of Syrian refugees in Jordan are from the southern part of Syria, many from a town called Daraa that is inhabited mostly by Sunni Muslims. While conducting my work in the field and through my interactions with Syrian refugees there, I saw how religion is integrated in everyday life practices, both inside and outside the workshop. This stands in contrast to secular urban centers like Damascus where some women wear Western-style clothes and children attend mixed-gender schools. In places like Zaatari, nearly all females wear hijabs, and men and women never shake hands. Further, there are constant references to Quranic verses in workshop conversation and even during breaks. Paradoxically, their attachment to conservative religious values did not prohibit them from participating in the workshop.

As a fellow Arab, I would imagine that members of the host community would be more interested in establishing a connection rooted in shared history, shared geography, and shared language rather than religion. However, this is not always the case. According to Brenda Oliden's (2015) thesis on the connection between religion and diaspora among Syrian refugees in Jordan, the practice of religion in Zattari Camp fosters a sense of belonging between Syrian refugees in the camp. She argues that transforming trailers into mosques created a sacred space that serves as a material manifestation facilitating a connection between the Syrian diasporic community and their homeland, as they decorate their trailers in a way that reminds them of their mosques back home.

I argue that, in the case of diasporic Syrians, religion becomes a factor that draws them together as a refugee community, and within the Arab world it can also connect them to the host community. The predominantly Islamic Jordanian community in this case is more accepting of Muslim refugees than Arab refugees of other religions. While speaking to many Jordanians, even those who oppose the Syrian refugee presence in Jordan, they would often end a conversation by saying "*akhwatna bildeen*," which translates literally as "our brothers and sisters in religion."

Despite the use of religious ornamentation to replicate home or the practice of religion as a cultural connection between refugees and their hosts, the fact remains that they are still strangers in their host communities.

Refugee as a stranger

Education researcher Jonnell Uptin (2013) describes the difference between a refugee and a stranger. Drawing upon the work Bauman (1991), Uptin analyzes the term *stranger* and distinguishes among different degrees of strangers and their usefulness to the host community. Uptin claims that while the immigrant and the guest worker come with "work readiness," refugees come with the expectation that they will lack the qualifications needed to immediately participate in the job market and thus that they will add an economic burden to the host community. In the middle of this useful discussion about how the average member of the host community perceives the refugee as a stranger, I argue for reflecting the refugee's side of the story.

During my work in one of the refugee centers in Berlin, I remember a lengthy conversation I had with a refugee woman in her 60s, who was a retired teacher from Syria and who had to take a boat from Turkey to Greece on the way to her final destination in Germany. When I confronted her with this argument, she shrugged it off by saying that Western European countries and Turkey are benefiting economically from extending the war in Syria, as many countries, including Germany and Sweden, are involved in arms trading that prolongs an already decade-long civil conflict. I remember her saying:

> If they want the war and refugee influx to stop, let them stop selling weapons. I am not here to look for home, I am here because I am

running away from home. My home which is destroyed by the West and the Europeans, and now they have the nerve to say whether they want us or not. They took my home from me. I barely remember it.

(Personal communication, 2015)

Her argument is not far from truth, nor is it an exaggeration, as many reports show evidence of arms trading (Knight, 2015; Staudenmaier, 2019). It may also help explain why many refugees are resistant to immersive integration and actually see the aid of the West as a Western responsibility for helping to perpetuate the very war the has left them displaced.

A six-year flood of Syrian refugees, beginning in 2011 and reaching its height in 2015 in Germany, stirred the pond of German politics. The arrival not only paved the way for both left- and right-wing political mobilization, but also opened the door of social activism within German society. New organizations were built, and many German people, especially retired ones who were feeling forgotten in their communities, suddenly found a meaning for their lives while volunteering and working as mentors for refugees. The arrival of citizens from Third World countries into the West allows for more social diversity and what political scientist Jeong- Won Park (2005, p. 204) refers to as the "duality" of the diaspora, where citizens from the diasporic community are in a position to be mediators between two cultures and should not be perceived as a threat to the host community.

Take the Syrian refugee community in Germany, for example; while the West is engaged in a frantic campaign to demonize Islam, the Syrian refugee communities, which are predominantly comprised of moderate Muslims, could use their position to act as mediators between Germans, and even Westerners in general, and Muslim communities. It is about time to move on and look at what unites us above what divides us. It is about time to accept the fact that the only constant principle is change. Park (2005, p. 10) argues that providing diasporic groups with a space to form their own distinctive identities does not threaten the host community's stability. Their increased stability could be achieved through developing a "positive sense of obligation as a citizen towards the host country."

The Syrian diasporic community possesses a sense of shared memory that is connected to the present refugee crisis and at the same time rooted in a shared historical narrative that was achieved through the Syrian educational apparatus. Schools in Syria, at least during the 1980s and '90s, used the same textbooks and followed a standardized curriculum of readings, poems, history lessons, etc. That shared cultural framework connected all Syrians before the war, and in the context of post-war displacement it combines with collective present memories of displacement to bond refugees within a singular group identity that any two Syrian refugees might feel

90   *Conclusion*

instinctively upon meeting. Trying to replace this Syrian/refugee identity with, let's say, a Germany identity is a futile endeavor. You can teach Syrians how to read and write in German, you can teach Syrians how to operate within German society, go to school, find work, and live, but you cannot ask Syrian refugees who have spent their formative years outside of Germany to wear a German identity.

This model of applied theater work is designed to foster emotional healing, in-group bonding, and the facilitation of dialogue with the host community. It is also structured to privilege individuals and their lived experience before displacement and within their current existence outside of their home country. Any work which seeks to erase the Syrian/Iraqi/Somali/etc. life and family from the refugee and to replace it with a new German or American identity will fail in its mission. When we set our sights on the whole person and self-fulfilling productivity within his or her new community, we may finally have a strategy for addressing refugees as people and not as a problem, and applied theater can do exactly this.

References

Alfonso, C., Kokot, W., & Tölölyan, K. (Eds.). (2016). *Diaspora, identity and religion: New directions in theory and research*. London: Routledge.

Bauman, Z. (1991). The social construction of ambivalence. In P. Beilharz (Ed.), *The Bauman reader*. Oxford, Boston: Wiley-Blackwell.

Betiang, L. (2010). Theater of rural empowerment: The example of living Earth Nigeria foundations community theater initiative in cross river state, Nigeria. *Research in Drama Education: The Journal of Applied Theater and Performance*, *15*(1), 59–78. doi:10.1080/13569780903481037

Bourdieu, P. (1986). The forms of capital. In J. Richardson (Ed.), *Handbook of theory and research for the sociology of education* (pp. 241–258). Westport, CT: Greenwood.

Bourdieu, P. (1989). Social space and symbolic power. *Sociological Theory*, *7*(1), 14–25. doi:10.2307/202060

Friedmann, J. (2002). *The prospect of cities*. U of Minnesota Press.

Ganz, M. (2011). Public narrative, collective action, and power. In S. Odugbemi & T. Lee (Eds.), *Accountability through public opinion: From inertia to public action* (pp. 273–289). Washington, DC: The World Bank. doi:10.1596/978-0-8213-8505-0

Gurney, C. M., & Means, R. (1993). The meaning of home in later life. In S. Arber & M. Evandrou (Eds.), *Ageing, independence and the life course* (pp. 119–131). London: Jessica Kingsley Publishers.

Kelly, P., & Lusis, T. (2006). Migration and the transnational habitus: Evidence from Canada and the Philippines. *Environment and Planning A: Economy and Space*, *38*(5), 831–847. doi:10.1068/a37214

Knight, B. (2015, October 21). Weapons go to conflict zones the money comes to Germany. *Deutsche Welle*. Retrieved from www.dw.com/en/weapons-go-to-conflict-zones-the-money-comes-to-germany/a-18798104

Mallett, S. (2004). Understanding home: A critical review of the literature. *The Sociological Review*, *52*(1), 62–89. doi:10.1111/j.1467-954x.2004.00442.x

Morsillo, J., & Prilleltensky, I. (2007). Social action with youth: Interventions, evaluation, and psychopolitical validity. *Journal of Community Psychology*, *35*(6), 725–740. doi:10.1002/jcop.20175

Oliden, B. (2015). *The Syrian refugees in Jordan: Negotiating diasporic identity through scared symbols* (dissertation). ProQuest, California State University, Long Beach.

Park, J.-W. (2005). *The national identity of a diaspora: A comparative study of the Korean identity in China, Japan and Uzbekistan* (dissertation). Retrieved from http://etheses.lse.ac.uk/id/eprint/1904

Poppe, W. (2010). *Habitus and the reasons and intentions for residential mobility and homeownership: A mixed-method study among former refugees in Buffalo* (dissertation). ProQuest, State University of New York.

Rooksby, E., & Friedmann, J. (2002). Place-making as project? Habitus and migration in transnational cities. In J. Hillier (Ed.), *Habitus: A sense of place* (pp. 299–316). London: Routledge.

Rousseau, C., Bencit, M., Gauthier, M.-F., Lacroix, L., Alain, N., Rojas, M. V., . . . Bourassa, D. (2007). Classroom drama therapy program for immigrant and refugee adolescents: A pilot study. *Clinical Child Psychology and Psychiatry*, *12*(3), 451–465. doi:10.1177/1359104507078477

Snyder-Young, D. (2011). "Here to tell her story": Analyzing the autoethnographic performances of others. *Qualitative Inquiry*, *17*(10), 943–951. doi:10.1177/1077800411425149

Staudenmaier, R. (2019, June 25). German firms sent weapons-grade chemicals to Syria despite sanctions – Report. *Deutsche Welle*. Retrieved from www.dw.com/en/german-firms-sent-weapons-grade-chemicals-to-syria-despite-sanctions-report/a-49355053

Tweed, T. A. (1997). *Our lady of the exile: Diasporic religion at a Cuban catholic shrine in Miami* Oxford: Oxford University Press.

Uptin, J. (2013). *A search for a new identity: Examining the journey of former refugee youths living in Australia* (Doctorate thesis). Retrieved from https://ro.uow.edu.au/theses/4017

Index

96   *Index*

University of Jordan 10
University of Minho, Portugal 2
University of the Arts, Philadelphia 3
Uptin, Jonnell 88

value of applied theater work 26–27,
    43–44, 52, 60, 71–72, 74; and
    integration 78–79; limitations of
    69–70
victimhood 34, 60

waiting in limbo 48, 53, 60; and
    bureaucracy 68–69, 83
Wannous, Saadalah 52
warm-up games 47, 55–56, 65
Wehle, Philippe 66
Westerners: and Arabs 4; and gender
    equality 13–14
"Withholding the Personal Story: Using
    Theory to Orient Practice in Applied
    Theater About HIV and Human
    Rights" (Cahill) 68
Wolf, Stacy 18
women: and conservatism 13–14,
    18–19, 20, 41–42, 52, 55, 87; and

empowerment 4, 6; and movement
    workshops 75–76; and personal
    narratives 26, 36–37, 38–39, 40;
    workshop participation in Jordan 6,
    42–43
women's rights 4, 19
"Writing and Righting Trauma:
    Troubling the Autoethnographic
    Voice" (Tamas) 73
"Writing Trauma: Collisions at the
    Corner of Art and Scholarship"
    (Tamas) 69

youth: and empowerment 31–32, 80;
    and gender 18–19, 41–42; and
    identity 39–40; and integration 81;
    and name monologue exercise 38;
    and victimhood 34; and Zaatari
    Camp 37, 43–44, 87

Zaatari Camp 10, 12–13, 87; and
    gender 41–42; and Jordanian host
    community 34; youth workshops in
    31–32, 37–40, 43–44
Zarqa 31, 37

For Product Safety Concerns and Information please contact our EU
representative GPSR@taylorandfrancis.com
Taylor & Francis Verlag GmbH, Kaufingerstraße 24, 80331 München, Germany